MW01248759

Bye Bye and Rocket Candies

VIGNETTES from the MAGIC of a child's early self-expression

Anthony Cook

Bye Bye and Rocket Candies

Rockets Candy® Is A Registered Trademark Of Rockets Candy Company, Newmarket, Ontario., Canada L3Y7B2

ISBN-13: 978-1490552712

ISBN-10: 1490552715

Published by Anthony Cook

For Amy and Alex and Lynn and Tony, with
        many fond memories of Scott and Danny
        .... Rub-a-dub-dub ....

And for everyone who has felt and known
        the magic of living with a little kid

- **Acknowledgments** -

"Dazed, goofy, frivolous." So reads a sign defining the word "silly". It was one of many signs along the Winnie the Pooh ride at Disney World, and I wrote it down and placed it in the latter part of Chapter 16. I knew this was a special word in my manuscript. This couple of pages is where one acknowledges and thanks many of the sources of inspiration and content in the work at hand, is it not? We're underway.

Going back to the beginning. I certainly want to acknowledge Meryl and Don Forrest – that's "Grandma" and "Grandpa" for the rest of the book. Thank you for everything you've done and continue to do. Thank you Peggy and Jim Blaiklock for your kind, fun hospitality at your lakeside home when my children were little kids (Chapter 12). Thanks Josie Mann for reminding me (when we visited your bookstore) of "The Great Gildersleeve" - a long ago radio program I listened to when I was a boy. Throckmorton, Mortimer – really. No wonder Alex thought you were a silly lady (Chapter 3). Thank you everyone who climbed aboard our steam train when my two kids were little. Didn't we have a wonderful time?

I would like to acknowledge and thank Glennis and Phil Cohen for kind words and early-on encouragement with my writing. Anne and AnDREW Olscher too. ("AnDREW" - Chapter 4). My profound thanks to James Holden Quinn, and his LifeStream program, which helped me to see my way clearly through the years. And son Ross too for the sequel. Thank you very much Ross.

In his classic book for children, **Love You Forever**, Robert Munsch wrote a little song: "I'll love you forever,
I'll like you for always,
As long as I'm living
my baby you'll be."

Well, one day my boy Alex came home from preschool and sang this song to me, except he changed the last two lines to "You'll be my baby, you'll be" (Chapter 3). Thank you Bob for understanding why Alex might have done this, and for allowing his one-time alteration to stand. And thank you for writing this very wonderful book.

In a similar vein, thank you Eric Ostrow of Rockets Candy Company. I don't think this Company has ever called them "rocket candies" as my young one did all along (Chapter 10). I know Alex never called them "Rockets". Thank you Eric for not minding. I don't think it mattered to Eric what my little boy called them as long as he liked them. He sure did. Hmm. Maybe that's why his toilet training took …. never mind.

I want to acknowledge the recent contributions to this project of the following people. Thank you very, very much.

Phil Jenkins – Phil shared his insight into the publishing industry as it sits today, and this was very helpful to a novice like myself.

Kae McColl – Kae, an experienced book editor, gave me a solid thumbs up after her careful review of the manuscript.

Mary Montague – It was thumbs down at the outset. ("A hundred and sixty pages about little kids? I don't think so.") Mary designed and created the cover, led me through the steps to create the file to upload, and – she read the book. ("It's a feel good, relaxing book that I enjoyed reading a lot.")

Anita Rutledge – I love the picture you took that is on the back cover: two little kids running into the covered bridge in Wakefield, Québec, I think that's mom and dad at the far end. "Messing about" – that's for sure.

Lynn, thank you for abiding my long hobby, my long distraction, my solitude. Thank you for the kids. Amy and Alex, thank you for your love and your company and I wish you well in everything you do. More than anyone, this book is for you.

Daddy Cook
(Chapter 3)

CONTENTS

- Introduction -

For those of us who have children, parenting is a very large dimension of our being. There are many phases. If you like, there's a pre-natal course to begin. Then the little one arrives. There's newborn. There's baby, toddler, little kid, kid, pre-teen, teen and others no doubt.

The "little kid" phase is special. It's discrete, brief, very important, and absolutely beautiful. It's even magical. It begins when your child first uses words for self-expression and ends two or three years later when the essential learning of basic words and concepts is complete. As often as not, it's the most emotionally fulfilling time in a parent's life. As well, never does "make the world a better place" resonate more than when you're messing about with your little one.

Of course it's sentimental to talk like this, but it is a very tender and sentimental time, full of laughing and mush. Moreover, the dependency is unique – life matters. **Bye Bye and Rocket Candies** is a celebration of this sentiment, and it captures the ambience of living with your child when your child is a little kid.

It will entertain you, you the reader, the parent. It will do this by reminding you of a brief, magnificent time in your life. Not possible? It was a blur, wasn't it, full of very busy days largely forgotten. But you won't be far along before you'll find yourself thinking, "Yes, this is what it was like." And then, back to that magical time you go.

It will be easy for you to remember. From one family to another, there is so much commonality to the attributes of early parenting. The activities are much the same, issues too. They're met by a fairly uniform little-kid personality. Piecemeal learning applies to all, and the ensuing parental response likely was as remarkable for you as it was for me. It will feel good for you to remember too, because a reminder can go straight to the heart.

The book is very emotional. There's laughter throughout and warm feelings expressed from beginning to end, and it's all very exciting. Being true to the spirit of little kids everywhere, how could it not be exciting? It's a very fun celebration.

PROLOGUE

Humour and warmth – that's why little kids are cute. Oh sure, those faces that sit on top of pudgy, awkward, free-wheeling limbs and bodies are particularly cute, and photo albums are filled with this cuteness. But there's so much more.

Take a little one and put it in motion. Teach it a few words, but only a little about each. Listen for some noise. Watch out for some action. A little expressiveness, a hugely underdeveloped personality, and soon and often you'll find yourself laughing out loud and feeling warm all over. This is the upside: humour and warmth. This is the joy of early parenting, and this is what the following is all about. It's a brief journey into that warm and wonderful time when your children are very young.

Amy's first few minutes

Let's go back four years and meet one of those little ones. Her name is Amy Elizabeth. She was born one evening in early April at Riverside Hospital in Ottawa, and once underway, she was washed, wrapped and handed to me. I'm her dad.

Cradling her in my arms, I looked down into her sweet face. Just a few minutes old, there she was, looking up at me. She was looking right into my eyes and I remember thinking it was a rather judgmental look. It was as if she was wondering if I was up to it, or perhaps, did she have a choice. I was looking at her with a smile, feeling quite proud and parental, and all the while – she was sizing me up. Then she fell asleep, I hope she wasn't bored.

They wheeled the bed off to a recovery area, not much more than a widening of the hall, and drew a curtain around. On the other side there was a lull in the comings and goings, and while Amy slept in her mother's arms, I sat down on the bed beside them. The bright hospital glare was gone. All was very still. Very quiet. For the first time, as our eyes rested on our tiny bundle, our brand new baby girl, a sense of the enormity of it all began to settle in. Suddenly tears came, and we cried and cried and cried.

And we went home – the three of us. It was only a day or two later, and soon after that I was back to work. Friends would drop by and say, "Congratulations Dad." I'd say, "Thanks," but I'd wonder. When a child is born, dad hasn't really done very much. He participated in the decision-making and thereby made a commitment. As the months went by, chances are he offered all sorts of moral support. But it was mom's pregnancy, her labour, and her discomforts. Mom is the deserving one, and I never have figured out "Congratulations Dad." I had a few days off and quite an exciting time.

The magic begins

It was very exciting. Lynn and I remember so well that early April visit to Riverside Hospital. We called it Amy's magic building because she did something very magical. She came out of the hospital, but nobody saw her go in! I thought about checking with Security, maybe asking a doctor or two, but I knew it was just a good trick. Well done Amy. The kid was barely a day old, and already – Daddy's wacko.

So it's a special building for us. We joke now and then about how that's where she did her magical "appearing" act, and we drive by and say, "Amy, there's your magic building." She's going to say, "You're nuts" any day now, and she'll be right – still wacko four years later.

Happy birthday, Amy!

Yes, it's four years ago today. It's time once again to say, "Happy Birthday sweetheart!" We love you so much Amy.

Her birthday party has been a long one. Today is Sunday and we came up to our cottage last night because we love being here for special times like birthdays. But her party began at home last Tuesday. Lynn's parents came over with their good wishes for Amy, they're out of town today. Madzy came by on Wednesday. She's a special friend, but wasn't sure she'd be able to drive up today.

In Ottawa, we live upstairs in a duplex. Lynn's sister Jane and her three daughters live downstairs. Can you imagine spending your first four years one flight of stairs above a loving aunt and three slightly-older cousins who, by and large, would trade their dolls for Amy in a second? It's been a non-stop deluge of love. They couldn't come to our cottage either, so Thursday was the day they had their party for Amy.

At last it's Sunday. When I wished her a happy birthday this morning she replied, "I'll be glad when my birthday's over." Too much front and centre I suppose. Well Amy, I'm sorry to say this, but don't forget your Tot-Romp party next Tuesday. Your downstairs cousins are coming, Stevie too. Lindsay's coming, and Kaitlyn and Larry and Rachel and Sydney and Tess and Vanessa and Ariana and…

*   *   *   *   *

…. Alex. He's coming for sure.

Alex is Amy's brother, seventeen months younger. So as Amy turns four he's on the older side of two-and-a-half. And he loves parties, he'll be there.

The downside

Two children, both so very young, so close in age – sounds wonderful, doesn't it. No? I remember a small, tired discussion with Lynn one evening a few days before Alex was born. We were trying to decide if our daughter's initials stood for "Amy Elizabeth" or "Atomic Energy". Which was it anyway? Then suddenly, Alex arrived and the question didn't matter anymore.

Yes, there is a downside and in a word, it's this: exhaustion. Back then, just keeping up with the routine needs and activity of young Alex and his not-much-older sister, Atomic Energy, was all-consuming. There are many other words – flustered, bored, sore, frustrated, baffled, angry, exasperated, to name just a few – and each has its moment in the sun. Shining brightly in the sunlight, exhaustion waits patiently at the door, ready to mix it up with all of them.

A little looking ahead helped me. Not long after Alex was born, I was very tired one night. For the fun of it, I sat down with a pencil and paper and drew two columns for each kid. I thought I'd note "target" and "actual" dates for a number of things to happen, and these I listed on the left.

They were things that, once achieved, would address my exhaustion problem. "Sleep through the night" was a big one. "Walk" was another, self-propulsion at last. Maybe the biggest of all was "toilet trained" and it was underlined, capital letters too. "Abandon infant crying", "crib to bed", "feed self" – there were several. "No more nursing" was big on Lynn's list. I added a final one last July when Amy was three: "Eat an ice cream cone on a hot summer day without needing a bath."

It was fun and I'd look at my notes from time to time, not that it really mattered. Just jotting down these relief milestones (who says they're "growth" milestones?) helped me to see ahead to when my fatigue might recede, assuming that there would be no third child. There would be no third child. If you have a little one right now, I'm sure you understand. Look out though. One thing that most certainly does not come with the upside is much time for reading. If you have two right now – well, never mind. With two, there's just no time for reading, no urge either, and you're not even here.

I'm exaggerating. The upside proceeds apace, of course it does. While some of the days are very long indeed, it's a time in your life you'll always remember as being altogether too short. One day quickly after another they fly by, and then they're gone.

Back to Riverside

Alex's arrival wasn't as dramatic as Amy's. I suppose that's to be expected, it was old hat to us now. We didn't cry, a second round of "Congratulations Dad" rolled off my back, and he never did size me up the way Amy did. I was watching though.

When we arrived at the hospital, I was watching for Joanne too and wondering if we'd see her again. Joanne was the nurse who helped Lynn right up until Amy was born. She was great – responsive, cheerful all the time. We had a big joke with her. Her shift ended at seven in the evening. Four o'clock came. Five o'clock. Six. Still no sign of Amy, hurry up Joanne. She hurried, and Amy was born at ten to seven! Phew.

We arrived about midnight. There she is! "Hi Joanne! Remember us? When are you finished this time? Seven in the morning? Okay, let's get started." Yes indeed, we had our joke all over again and this time, Alex showed up at six-forty-five. That was fun!

All through the long nighttime hours, her cheerfulness helped so much. There was lots of time to tell her about our 17-month-old princess; she hadn't seen her since her beginning so there was lots to tell. We talked. We laughed. We were very happy when Alex was born that early September morning. Especially Mom – happy to have it all behind her, happy to greet our newborn boy.

Alex is two and a half now, and when we drive by the hospital, is it his "magic building" too? No, just Amy's. He's going through his "It's mine" stage, and lays claim to just about everything that might possibly be his in any way at all. I don't think it's in me to listen to Amy and Alex argue about whose hospital it is.

One last look at the downside

We're waking up a little less tired these days, and there are several dates written down on my list. Yes, they do learn to sleep through the night – how blissful, how novel. They do begin to walk – my chiropractor misses me. They even eventually become toilet trained – boys too. So I'm told, that is. Somehow, the exhaustion has become more acceptable and we've learned to smile again.

One night a month or so ago, Alex was poking around all over Lynn's face, wanting to know the names of just about everything. Eyelids, eyelashes, eyebrows – he had trouble with the "brows" because he's fair and couldn't find his. He thought they were near the top of his forehead. Then he poked just below her eyes and Lynn said "cheek", but Alex wouldn't buy that. He knew where "cheek" was, and that wasn't it. Lynn said, "Okay, how about bags under the eyes?" That was fine. Now Lynn's afraid that whenever Alex talks about facial parts around the eyes – lashes, lids, brows, and bags – everyone will think it was his exhausted mother who taught him. And it was.

A few days ago at dinnertime Amy said, "Daddy, will you feed me?" Mommy was particularly tired that evening, but she immediately took up the question. "That's my girl! Four going on two, I'm so proud of her. She has such a good ability to delegate." When Dad's tired, he mopes and doesn't say much, but with Mom you just never know when a little humour might come forth. Or is this a little sarcasm. I'm tired, I prefer humour.

All aboard!

Amy's four – it hardly seems so. Our lives have been a wonderful blur since that magical appearing act of hers. She showed up and that was that. How could four years have gone by so fast!

I want to take you along on a trip and share this blurry experience with you. It's going to be exciting. The "upside" is so much fun – not just once in awhile when humour bests exhaustion, but constantly. Our train is about to depart. It's a steam train, plenty fast enough for our little passengers. Plenty fun enough too – do you hear the steam whistle? *How can you not hear the steam whistle!* Are you ready, do you have your bag?

It could not have been a more glorious first week of April for Amy to turn four. Her birthday finally has ended and we're soon to pull away. We'll roll gently down the track through the spring and summer months and on into early September. That's when we'll arrive at another birthday. Alex will be three this year, and that will be our last stop. We'll climb down off our train and head straight for his party, maybe three or four parties – just like Amy. And we'll say goodbye sadly because our magnificent train ride will be over.

Amy is becoming quite a talker these days. She says more and more all the time that is fun and noteworthy. So says her dad anyway. These little conversations will appear throughout because they're special. They're as close as we're apt to get to a semblance of maturity, what with young Alex running around on almost every page. They're very special.

Often though, they won't be connected very well to what comes before or after. That's all right, our family reality is like that too. The clickety-clack of the train won't bother her, she'll just talk louder. I can hear her now: "ALL ABOARD?" Or if she chooses to delegate to Alex – **"ALL ABOARD!!!"** Would Alex ever love to go to a train station and holler that.

So, this is a story about a brief time in the lives of an early four-year-old and a late two-year-old. But it's more than that. It's about laughing and mush, and those wonderful, joyous moments that fill the first months and then years of a child's life. It's about a very special love that begins abruptly, takes root, and grows warmly like the spring and summer seasons of our trip. Its blossoms are the best. Quickly they're in full bloom and forever they last.

Hop on and let's go.

PART I

SPRINGTIME IN OTTAWA

1

Meet Scott and Danny

Our two golden retrievers were on the train from the beginning, and one needs to say "Thank you" to them. They were nicely into middle age when Amy was born. That old adage, "You can't love a puppy too much", was about to be severely compromised, transposed actually. It became, "You can't love a child too much." Since both are met generally by allotting time, something had to give. Having to share Lynn and me with our newborn would require adjustment.

Scott is the older of the two. More descriptively, we often call him "Gagawagger". Danny, a female, is ten months younger. The kids have learned a great deal from these two, and they've grown to love the dogs as much as Lynn and I do. Many are the times we'd head off to the park – two leashes in one hand, Amy in her wagon in the other, Alex in his backpack, and off we'd go. We were a spectacle. Now both kids walk and that's easier for me. I said to Alex after one of these walks –

"Do you remember those other two dogs? They sure were barking a lot."

"They were going to come and bite us."

"No no, they wouldn't do that."

"They were going to just give me a kiss."

Lots of kisses for the kids, that's for sure. And no bites. Amy and I had a little talk about Scott one day. There was something very important that I wanted her to understand.

Sometimes Gagawagger would show up, tail wagging – actually his whole hindquarters wagging – with almost anything in his mouth. I told her that it's particularly important to keep socks away from him. If he had a sock and you didn't pay attention to him, he'd lie down, chew it, swallow it, and you'd never be able to wear it again. Amy said –

"Yes you could."

"How?"

"Just cut him."

"You mean cut him open and pull out the sock?"

"Yes. And tape him together again."

So you can see there was much to be learned with the dogs around. This time it was a use for tape. I'm relieved she was mindful of the need to fix Scott following his surgery.

Other times, there was considerable exposure to fundamental male-female differences. One can imagine. Most noticeably, this would happen when one or the other or both would be lying spread eagle on the floor with legs sticking up and out in all sorts of directions. Even young Alex noticed the difference, and this was quite evident in a little talk he and I had one day. He had a question about it. Danny was flat on her back sleeping, Alex pointed to her back end, and then he asked me –

"What's that?"

"That's her peeper."

"Where's her other peeper?"

That was the end of our talk. I didn't have an answer for his question so we went to the kitchen for a snack. Thank you Scott and Danny, thank you for moving over – not over and out, just over. You've adjusted beautifully.

*   *   *   *   *

Then there are Lynn and I, we're still working on adjusting. Our family used to be us two and two big dogs. Now we're six with two different kinds of children. So we're still adjusting. We've long been seasoned dog owners, now we're trying hard to become just as good at parenting. But we haven't been at it long enough it seems.

"Seasoned parents" is a phrase whose relevance creeps in by way of observation of others. Here we are, having the time of our lives, both enjoying and struggling, totally topsy-turvy. Then we see another mom and dad: calm, in control, quiet, very content, kids behaving beautifully – not unlike Scott and Danny in fact. Oh well.

Actually, there aren't six of us, there are seven these days. Yes, there's another, and you should meet her too before we're far down the track because she'll be aboard the entire trip.

One more family member

Amy wasn't even a year old when we bought her a doll. Doesn't every little girl want one? It was a very typical doll, nothing exciting but pretty. It was one of those dolls whose eyes closed when it lay down and opened when it sat up and Amy seemed to like it very much for a day or two, but then ignored it. A couple of weeks later, we brought it out for her again, and again her interest lasted only a short while. A few weeks later – same thing. Lynn and I spent more time playing with it than Amy did.

When she began to talk, she never mentioned her doll, never gave it a name, and never took it from its place in the corner of her bookshelf. Nor was she attached to any other toy. It seems she was just too interested in everything else her new life had to offer, including of course, her little brother.

Then last fall, Alex started to use words too, and right away expressed a liking for this doll. It was one of the first things he "talked" about – not too many words, just enough. So Amy gave it to him. He liked the clothes, a nightgown that suggested to all of us that the doll was a "her" and not a "him". He liked the big blue eyes that opened and closed. The eyelids were big too, and black, and this was why he named her "Blacks Eyes". Almost three years from when she first arrived in our house, Blacks Eyes finally had a home. She had a dad too – Alex. He's not a seasoned dad of course, he's not even a seasoned kid.

That's it for our all-the-way passengers: Lynn, me, two kids, a couple of dogs and a doll. No more. Our train is going faster now. There will be visitors as we travel through the summer months, and you'll meet them too. Other unseasoned kids will climb aboard at one stop or another. Parents too, and if I don't make strides at becoming less of an unseasoned parent, hopefully I'll notice how I'm not alone.

*   *   *   *   *

One visitor needs a special introduction right now. If this was a winter trip, she'd be with us all the way too. It's not though, and we'll miss her in the summertime when we move to the cottage. It's Aunt Jane.

With her young brood, she's our model seasoned parent and has played a very important part in our lives these last four years. We call it "Jane's daycare". Let me tell you what happened there one day this spring. It was right after Amy's birthday, our train had just pulled out. It was not good. It was significant, and for a moment derailment was a distinct possibility. What a way to begin a trip. But Aunt Jane stayed cool the whole while, and it soon became nothing more than a memorable blip in a little boy's early self-expression.

School's out

It happened down the street at Hopewell Avenue Public School. With Amy and Alex in tow, Jane arrived about a quarter to twelve to pick up Kelly, her youngest. Her half-day of kindergarten ended at noon. She had a few minutes, so she sat down on a bench in the hall to wait. A friend came and sat beside her, and with four-year-old Amy on her lap, she turned to her friend for a chat. They talked about Amy's birthday parties, and – where was Alex all this time? He was with her too, but he was on her other side, standing on the bench, looking at the wall, looking at all the kids' pictures on the wall, and looking at whatever else the wall had to offer. Such as the fire alarm button. Alex could just reach it if he stood on his tiptoes, and since its only reason for being there was to be pushed, he obliged.

The phone rang and it was Lynn. "Oh no, he didn't!" All sorts of things flashed through my mind. How's Alex, what will I say to him? Poor Jane! Should I talk to the Principal? Maybe I better go home. "Poor Jane" flashed through my mind a couple of times actually. I calmed down. I smiled and settled back to work because it wasn't anywhere near quitting time.

Yes, I smiled. Picture Jane sitting there, pleasantly chatting with her friend. Suddenly she hears the alarm and thinks to herself: "Oh my goodness, that's the fire alarm", followed by a slowly growing awareness that maybe the little blond boy beside her – the one standing on the bench, the one who just turned around rather abruptly and lowered his arm at the same time, the one named Alex – maybe he did it. A slowly growing awareness and nowhere to hide. Quickly she was immersed in embarrassment and cover-up, and very distracted from her two charges. That's okay, it's not as if there was another button around for him to push. She told me later that right when it happened, she noticed for the first time that a smelly diaper had just materialized. She thought for an instant that this might be why everyone was running out of the school. Comic relief. Really Jane, change the diaper. Then she did some more thinking to herself: "This can't be happening to me." She sent a note to the Principal and headed home with Alex and Amy; and Kelly, she didn't forget Kelly. Good for her.

There were many reactions to what the little blond boy did. What an unusual day! What about Alex, was he upset? Not much. He was a little frightened by the noise and the rush, but very much unaware that it was his doing. To him it was just one more goings-on that he'd come to understand some day, no hurry.

A few days later, Jane and her small entourage ran into Lauren when she was with several of her classmates. Ten-year-old Lauren is Jane's oldest. She told me afterwards that they all wanted to meet Alex. "Hey, there's the kid who pushed the fire alarm!" "Wow! Is he brave!" "Cool dude!" "Awesome!" They were impressed.

The school Principal wasn't impressed at all. She read Jane's note, and that afternoon turned on the public address system and said that a "two-year-old preschooler couldn't resist the shiny red button on the wall. Someday, he'll grow up and know not to do things like this." Now how would she know that? Hmm. I wonder if a Principal has ever tripped the fire alarm just for the heck of it. You know – stress, a wandering sense of humour. Making presumptions about my boy? Not allowed.

Kristen is nine, the middle one of the three. What did she think of it all? I never would have known had Alex not commented a day or two later –

"I got Kristen out of school, I did."

"How did you do that?"

"I just pushed the button."

Now we know how Kristen reacted – she had a little talk with her young cousin. Kristen understands cause and effect. None of this "....couldn't resist the shiny red button...." stuff for her. She told Alex exactly what happened, and in a way that suggested to him that this was something to brag about. Speaking of which, how did Dad react?

I think Dad did not react too much. However. How many people do you know who have managed to bring fire trucks screaming and empty an 800-student school before their third birthday? Well, my son Alex DID IT!!

That evening, Lauren, Kristen and Kelly all came running to the bus stop. "Did you hear what happened at school today?" "Did you hear what Alex did?" I said yes, I know, and I headed straight to Jane, poor Jane. I gave her a big hug. I quietly said to her, "Thanks Jane. Thanks for letting it happen." Jane said she thought she detected some parental pride. Nonsense.

When it was all over, Jane carried on with her daycare. Yes, she's seasoned all right, more than most. Otherwise she would have been knocked out by this one I should think. Such stress, yet such composure – we're sure going to miss her this summer.

*   *   *   *   *

Becoming a seasoned parent

It happens and you saw it. Or maybe you didn't see it happen but you should respond anyway. You need to assess. Then you need to do something, or praise or punish or forget that anything happened in the first place. It's complicated, there's so much to learn and it's all part of becoming a seasoned parent. It begins early.

Conversations, or lack thereof, with an almost-one-year-old

Amy had a rattle that she liked a lot. It was a big plastic key ring with three brightly coloured keys. It was easy to hang on to – when she wanted to – and on a long walk in her backpack, she'd often carry it all the way. I would tell her to shake it every once in awhile to let me know she was still there.

One time, she was sitting on my lap playing with her keys and dropped them on the floor. I picked them up and talked to her about them –

"I like these keys Amy, do you?"

She said nothing. I went on –

"This one's for your car, this one's for your office, and this one's for the back door so you can sneak in when you come home late at night. Okay?"

Same response, she might not have been listening. So I handed them back and this time, she threw them on the floor.

Actually, I think she threw them there the first time too, she didn't drop them at all. I wasn't sure though, and did it really matter? Too young? Maybe if she was four or five, "dropping" would be okay but "throwing" not. Or would it be the other way around?

I remember one evening when Alex was almost two. He picked up the top of a crystal butter dish and held it out over the kitchen floor. He was sitting in his little chair, securely fastened to the table, but the butter dish wasn't fastened to anything. Too bad.

What to do. I could yell at him. If he was older, that's probably what I would do. Or I could say nothing, and just carry on with a rather helpless, startled look on my face. I could politely ask him to put it back on the table. Please. I knew I didn't have much time. I began to approach the table very slowly, saying softly, "Alex be very careful with that it's quite expensive please hang on to it tightly and if you don't drop it I'll love you forever." I was almost at the table. I carefully reached out, and…. Smash. He laughed. He thought the noise was funny.

Guilty or not-guilty? Hmm. Anything to say here? What would you do? Questions, questions, questions. Somebody once said, "If you're gonna have kids, you're gonna pay for it." Little kids come with price tags all over them.

One late winter day close to Amy's birthday, I had a question. There was an incident. It snowed in the morning, but after lunch it was warm and beautiful under the afternoon sun. We opened some windows and I could hear two little ones playing in the backyard. They were having fun until something happened all of a sudden. Alex began to cry. Quickly, I came to the door – he had fallen off the picnic table bench where he had been sitting beside Amy. Here's what I heard of their talk before they saw me –

"Alex, you still love me don't you?"

"Yeah, I love you Amy."

"I didn't push you, you just fell."

"Yeah, I fell. It hurts still."

She pushed him. Right? Oh. Not right. It's just a little thing, but there's no replay and you wish there was. Well, what do you think? Maybe she just pushed him a little bit.

It begins early, you learn a little more every day. When are you finally there? Here's a test. You know you're a seasoned parent when a sudden very loud scream can confidently be ignored. You're not seasoned when you ignore it but you really shouldn't have. Rather basic, isn't it. No, I don't think I'm ever going to be seasoned. Ask me thirty years from now when I have twenty-five more kids.

2

Late winter in Ottawa is a time of contrasts. It can be very wet with snow melting as the weather warms. Then it can be quite cold, and as the anticipation of spring is put off for not too long, one hopes, a warm fire is inviting. An extra hour or two under the covers on a chilly weekend morning is enticing.

It can be lots of fun for little ones outside. The wetness freezes and you never have to look far to find a little slide. Perhaps there was some ice at the picnic table and Alex slid off the bench. No, he was pushed. I think so.

Conversations with a four-year-old

It was this year around her birthday when Amy seemed to learn what "melting" meant. It was happening all over the place. One day in the car, we were talking about the last clumps of snow sitting on the canal along our way. Amy had it figured out and here is what she said –

"Do you know what happens when snow melts?"

Well yes, I do know. So I told her –

"It turns into water."

"No."

"What happens then?"

"It goes THROUGH the water, and lands on the fishes."

"Who told you that?"

"Just me."

Amy has a special little friend named "Just me". I wonder what else her friend has been telling her.

That Saturday, it was cold again. Bed was the place to be and Lynn wanted to sleep in a bit. However, Amy and Alex both decided to climb in with her, so more sleep would be difficult. Sure enough, it wasn't long before Alex began to behave like an orangutan. To his credit, he was quiet. Maybe he knew he wasn't supposed to make noise if someone was sleeping. There's more to know about that, isn't there. Lynn never had a chance. He was standing, sitting, rolling, bumping – he was all movement. Amy had an idea –

"Mommy, why don't you call a polar bear to come and eat him?"

It wasn't quiet anymore. Mommy said –

"Let's lie down and snuggle and go back to sleep for a little bit."

And what did wide-awake Alex have to say about that? He had a concern actually –

"What about the polar bear?"

And nobody went back to sleep. A dog, another dog, an orangutan, a polar bear – so goes our menagerie.

*   *   *   *   *

At our cottage, winter is wonderland. It's very quiet and white, right from the first snowfall. We often go there on weekends as it's only an hour from Ottawa. That's where we have our fireplace and a warm fire on a Friday night is wonderful.

If it had snowed much since our last visit, there would be shoveling to do. Often, I'd not quite finish the long driveway before I'd find myself thinking about when the kids would be big enough to handle a shovel. Sometimes, if it was warm and then cold, or if there was some freezing rain, the country roads would be very slippery. From time to time each winter, we'd have to be careful driving. That's all though. The weather never kept us from going to the cottage, and once there, it never kept us from going home – nor from going out to the store to buy Saturday's newspaper.

A winter drive in the country

One polar-bearish day in January a couple of years ago, off we went for the paper. Amy and I. Of course she would come along. A bit short of her second birthday, she loved these trips to the store. This time, there was ice on the road so I would have to go slowly. The snow banks were plowed high on each side and it would be like driving in a trough. There would be some hills, small ones, and likely no other cars along the way.

It was beautiful outside that day – so still, so winter white. Faded red barns, evergreen thickets, bare black branches, empty deep blue sky and golden sun – I was sure I was in wonderland – wide white rolling fields broken by jagged country fences. I loved it.

I drove slowly. We crawled, Amy and I. My seat belt was fastened tightly, and Amy was all buckled up in her car seat behind me. About a mile along the way we came to the first hill. It wasn't very big, and I went just a little faster to make it all the way up. We made it, up and over, and then – very, very slowly….oh oh. Wrong. Faster again. It mattered not that my foot was on the brake, we were on our way down!

The car slid right around and faced uphill – it was going backwards! It nudged the snow bank on the left. Then it kept turning, right around again and nudged the snow bank on the right – or was it the left one again. Who cares, this was so dramatic, I don't drive down hills this way! Another turn, uphill again, and finally – finally, it stopped at the bottom.

I took a deep breath. I quickly looked back at Amy expecting to see a frightened, tearful face, very much in need of comforting. When she caught my eye, which was not right away, she gave me an ear-to-ear grin, and all she said was –

"Wheeeee."

Winter carousel! One word, a grin, did I ever feel better! Who needed the comforting? It was me. Amy was fine, she was too young to be afraid. I bet she was hoping I had more tickets so we could do the ride again. No more tickets Amy, let's go buy some candy floss. All in a day at the fair.

*   *   *   *   *

In my brief four-year exposure to my children, I've come to think that the most typical aspect of little-kid behaviour is the unexpected. Short lives have yet to teach what's normal, so the door is open to imagination. You see it in the things they do, you most certainly hear it in so many of the things they say. Perhaps this is why seasoned parenting seems out of reach.

Alex was concerned the other morning when he asked, "What about the polar bear?" You wouldn't expect that to come from Lynn's suggestion that they snuggle and sleep a little more, would you? I wonder what he was thinking. Was he hoping to see a polar bear? Or did he want to play with one, maybe jump around on the bed with it. Or did he think that since it was coming to eat him, Mommy would protect him, and there might be a problem if Mommy was asleep. What was going on in his mind, how much had he heard – how much did he understand? You have to wonder. It's not obvious from where his question came and as a result, it's unexpected.

Amy surprised me when she said what she did after our spin-around on the icy road that beautiful day in January two years ago. It was a happy surprise, and there have been many since. Let's go back to our wonderland – another winter, another very little kid.

A year later at Vorlage

The two of them and I were at the cottage for a few days. It was January again. Alex was almost one and a half now, and he wasn't using words very much, not even simple ones like "Whee". His expression was all behaviour.

One day while we were there, we went for a drive and his behaviour was very typical. He did something quite unexpected. Not only that, it was most unique – what a special boy I thought. I had never seen anyone, any age, do this before or since, and I doubt that I ever will. I still smile when I think about it.

It was a cold, cloudy morning and we headed off. Around eleven, we all felt hungry and I had a good idea. We'd go to Vorlage for lunch. Unfortunately, I wasn't fully equipped for restaurant dining. I had the most dangerous problem area covered – spare diapers – but I didn't have any bibs or sipper lids. One could expect a little spillage.

Alex was amazing with sipper lids. These are lids for a cup that have a narrow spout that controls the outflow. Put one of these on a cup, and Alex could whip it up and into his mouth in half a second and he wouldn't spill a drop. Rather good motor skills, would you not agree? Imagine. If he whips it up too slowly or stops just short of his mouth – all over his shirt. On the other hand, if he flips it back too hard, he gets a nose or mouth full of cup. Ouch! Of course, he'd had a lot of practice doing it more deliberately, with a lot of spilling too.

Vorlage is a ski lodge, and it was early enough that there would not be very many in the restaurant. We would be able to find a table by a window and watch some skiing. Never before had Amy or Alex seen anyone ski, so this would be fun.

There was no one there at all. We had the run of the place, so to speak. Alex could attest to that. We grabbed some lunch – two bowls of pea soup, two apple juices, a pop and a hot dog for me – and sat down to eat and watch. I'd tell them quietly something like "Look at how fast they're going. Wow!" Amy would shout –

"Don't go too fast! Be CAREFUL! Don't fall!"

As they approached the bottom, not many fell. They might have heard her. Alex and I sure did, and indeed, we had a very fun time.

I had removed the foil top from Alex's apple juice. While Amy was telling the skiers to be careful, I found myself thinking – Alex, you be very careful. I watched him closely all the while. But he wasn't interested in his apple juice. He was restless, and being a toddler – only a year and a half – when he finished his pea soup, he toddled off to check out a salt shaker at one table, some napkins at another.

It happened very quickly. Amy had called me away from our table to look at something and in this moment of distraction, Alex returned for his juice. He reached up, put both his little hands on the cup, lifted it off the table for a moment, and then with all the grace and savvy of a master, threw all the apple juice straight into his very own face. SPLASH! None went over his head, none went by his ears – he was so good at it!

Poor Alex. He didn't cry, maybe he found it refreshing. Maybe he drank some of it, that was his intention. Maybe he felt that the sensation – wet, cold, sticky? – was non-offensive and just a part of everyday life. Maybe that's what he thought. When I think about it, I still smile, and no – I really doubt I'll ever see that happen again.

*   *   *   *   *

Conversations with a four-year-old

Amy didn't learn about melting all at once. While driving alongside the canal a couple of weeks ago, I explained to her that when snow melts, it turns into water. She countered with something about it landing on fishes, so I don't know what she learned there.

Anyway, here we were sitting in the kitchen having some ice cream, and she said –

"We better eat this quick or it's going to melt."

Hey, good learning! It's going to melt. Yes, yes, yes. I asked –

"What happens when it melts?"

"It turns into water."

It turns into water. Oh well. "Just me" might have been the one to tell her that too, so I wasn't about to argue. Wait a minute. Wasn't it her dad who told her that? "Just me" said it lands on fishes. Patience Dad. Maybe Amy's not quite ready to take on melting ice cream.

- **3** -

I saw quite a bit of Alex's approach to throwing his drink in his own face, didn't I. Yes I might have been able to stop him, there was a moment. But I didn't. Now isn't that an interesting reaction. I suppose some day, with all due conscience, I'll be accountable for that choice. That's okay, I have between now and then to figure out what to tell him. "I'd just taken a big bite of my hot dog", "Actually, I didn't see it at all", "Served you right, squirt, for breaking my butter dish". I'll think of something.

I like to call him "squirt" now and again. I never used to when he was a toddler and acted his age regularly, but nowadays – I do. It's fun. He always winds up as though he's really going to let me have it. I don't know why. He is a bit small and I explain that to him. I tell him, "Alex, I call you 'squirt' because you're smallish but that's okay, you haven't been around long enough to grow very much." He winds up anyway, and I disarm him with a scratch on the tummy where he's ticklish.

I never call him that when he's drinking something. His learning about sipper lids took a big step that day. Not only is he a master at delivery, but he's learned to look first. Just the other day, I gave him some apple juice and said –

"Here's your apple juice. Now please don't spill any."

"Because it's got a lid on it."

What a good boy.

*   *   *   *   *

However, most of the name-calling has come from the kids, which is entirely to be expected. So much of this first learning has to do with attaching names to things. And to people, dogs, dolls, and even themselves – it's so fun. Then comes the re-naming.

Alex likes his own name – "Christopher Alexander Cook". We all like it. Grandma likes it too, but she had a problem. She knew someone well named Alexander who was always called "Alec" for short. She'd often forget and call our little boy "Alec". He noticed this, and one time when there were several people in the room, including Grandma, someone asked him what his name was. In a very matter-of-fact way, he said –

"My name is Alex, Grandma call me Alec."

We all laughed. Grandma too, and she never called him Alec again. Good learning there.

Indeed, Grandma was a big help in teaching him the difference between "Alex" and "Alec". But she left the difference between "Alex" and "Alexander" to Lynn and I, and it wasn't easy. His first response was denial –

"Well, I'm not AlexANDER, I'm Alex COOK."

Then came confusion. One day, I referred to him as a young fellow, but then thought I'd better check –

"Can I call you 'Young fellow'?"

"No."

Good thing I checked.

"Then can I call you 'Old man'?"

"No."

"Well, what can I call you?"

" 'Christopher Alex Zander Cook', that's my whole name."

Actually, he wasn't confused, he was sure that was his whole name. You could tell by the inflection in his voice as he said each of his four names separately and distinctly. One tries.

Kiki, Jock, Broccoli, Dope, and Diaper

I wanted to teach him about relationships, I wanted him to know that he was my "son". So we had a few little talks over two or three days. I worked hard on "daddy" and I think he was beginning to understand. He certainly was coming, at last, to know his own name very well –

"My name is Alexander Cook."

"My name is Tony Cook."

"Well, you're Daddy Cook. You don't like me to call you Tony."

I worked harder.

"Only two people can call me Daddy. You're one of them. Do you know who the other one is?"

"Amy. And who's the other one that can call you Tony?"

Okay. So now we'll work on "Tony". Alex informed me –

"Your name is Tony. You're a little Tony, but you're very long."

"Mommy calls me Tony. Aunt Jane, Grandpa, Uncle Dave, they all call me Tony. Everybody can call me Tony. But you, and Amy, are the only ones who can call me Daddy. And you're the only one whom I can call my son."

"And me call Blacks Eyes 'Kiki'!"

And he was off. He had an excited grin on his face, and he told me how he called his mommy "Jock", and Kendra "Broccoli", and Madzy "Dope", and Amy "Diaper". He laughed and laughed and laughed. I don't think I'll teach him that he's my son anymore, maybe I'll feel like it some other time. Squirt.

*　　*　　*　　*　　*

A few more days and all the snow will be gone. Soon there will be green grass, budding trees – tulips everywhere! Ottawa is beautiful as white becomes green in the springtime, as cold becomes warm and flowers fill your eyes with colour.

Amy enjoyed the snow going away this year. She knows now that it turns into water even though ice cream doesn't, and it's April so it's melting. But it's also today, and today it's snowing with big white, wet flakes and only a few. She was absolutely gleeful this morning –

"Guess what. It's melting, but look. It's snowing out! How can that be!"

Cackle, cackle, cackle. When Amy is excited and thinks something is funny, she "cackles", and that's the only word to describe it. I love it. It's one of those many noises that little kids make that catch your ear and remind you that there's a child at large here.

Audible moments

Giggling is another one – you hear it all the time. One night I was doing the dishes and Amy came running into the kitchen.

"Daddy, guess what. I have the giggles."

So she did, and it continued for some time. I checked in the living room and saw why right away – there on the floor was a "mommy sandwich". The giggling was coming from the bottom slice, Alex was on top. A moment or two later I heard another voice. This one was quiet, unconcerned, adult. "Dad, I'm getting mutilated." No urgency, information only.

I did some more dishes, and then –

"Daddy, would you come here for a minute? I want to show you my trick. It's a very funny one."

I went into the living room again, and Amy was lying on the couch. When she saw me, she rolled off onto the floor and carried right on rolling across the carpet, giggling all the way.

More giggling a little later, and when I went back to investigate, I didn't see her right away. I saw an upside-down plastic laundry hamper with Alex sitting on top of it watching television. I could hear her though – she was under the hamper. She was giggling, but I thought I detected a little impatience, maybe a little annoyance. The giggling was about to come to an end and be put aside for another time.

The little boy on the hamper would entertain us almost every day with some incidental humming. The tune would be one of those totally-never-heard-by-anybody ones, and he'd stop for a breath not at the end of a line, but when he needed a breath. Wait a minute. There were no lines. This musical accompaniment was adorable as he went about his play.

Sometimes, there would be words, and one would hear a complete composition. One day in early May, first Jane and then I were exclusive audiences to such presentations.

For a week or two we had noticed that Alex was making too frequent use of a four-letter word beginning with "k" and ending with a double consonant. It wasn't "kiss". It was suggested that he might stop doing this, then it was requested that he cease, and then he was told to stop. Then he was told again to stop. We told him over and over, etcetera, again and again, and then one day he stopped. The next day, when Jane picked him up at the end of his preschool, he climbed into her car and it was very quiet. With just the two of them there, he turned to Jane and said, "Would you like to hear my new song?" Later she told me it was sweet and beautiful the way Alex spoke to her at that moment. She didn't start the car, but turned to him and was all set to enjoy one of the softer moments of being with a two-year-old. "Yes I'd love to hear it." Alex, with a beautiful, quiet little home-made tune, looked out the front window and began –

"I – am – going – to – kill – you,
I – am – going – to – bump – you."

That was the matinee. His evening performance was more memorable. When I lay down with him at bedtime, he had another new song. I wish I could have remembered the tune but there was no way. It was another original. The words were special –

"I'll – love – you – forever,
I'll – like – you – for – always,
You'll – be – my – baby, – you'll – be."

I'll for always remember these words. Some day, if a little anger comes between Alex and me, I'll pretend he knew exactly what they all meant. He didn't, of course. Maybe generally, but not the nuances, and that's what made it special.

A few days later, I discovered that his collection of words wasn't quite as original as his tune. He'd remembered them from his preschool reading earlier in the day. He altered the third line though, and added an extra "You'll be". After all, he wanted to be very clear when he sang the words to his dad. I'm the one. Not Aunt Jane. Me. Quite a difference in content between his song for her and his song for me, wasn't there. Poor Jane.

Don't think for a moment he doesn't love his Aunt Jane dearly, he just doesn't know words well yet. But humming? He knows that very well and he loves it. He hums a lot.

Conversations – with music – with a four-year-old

Amy's interest in music these days is more traditional. She likes to listen to it. Dad and Mom say it's a good thing to do, they do it, so she does it. Does she have a favourite song? She has a favourite friend, a favourite colour, many other favourites too. She even told me once that I was her favourite dad. Of course she has a favourite song. And another favourite song, and another.

Her favourite song has ranged from "Pop goes the weasel" to the third movement of Chopin's Piano

Concerto in E Minor about which she commented one Saturday morning at breakfast when it was playing in the background: "I like this song. It's my favourite."

One day we were listening to one of Amy's tapes in the car, and the song was "The Yellow Rose of Texas". I told her –

> "Amy, that used to be my dad's favourite song and when I was a little boy, he'd sing it to me."

"It's my favourite song too."

Then when the song was over and the next one started, she added –

> "This one's my favourite favourite song."

And Amy's my favourite favourite favourite daughter. So there.

There are all sorts of audible moments: cackling, giggling, humming, songs (all favourites should you happen to ask), and "chortling", just to name a few. Alex chortles when he talks about the silly lady he met who calls him Mortimer.

There's a little bookstore not far from the cottage, and Alex and I dropped in one Saturday. There were many children's books and a very nice lady who looked after it all. While I was shopping in one part of the store, she and Alex were having a grand time in another. They were laughing and laughing, and when we were home again, Alex said –

"The silly lady in the store calls me Mortimer."

That's when he chortled.

We went back another day and she called him Mortimer again. I asked her why, and she looked me in the eye and told me very seriously that Alex had objected when she had called him Throckmorton.

So that's why. What a silly lady. It's no wonder he chortles when he thinks of her.

First, it was "Alex". Then it was "Alec", "AlexANDER", "Zander", "Alexander", "Daddy", "Tony", and Alex was bored. So it was on to "Kiki" and "Jock" and so on. That reminded me of "squirt" again. Now it's "Mortimer", not "Throckmorton", but "Mortimer". So many names – they're important all right.

This land is your land,
This land is my land, ...

Alex has been in a preschool program since January. Amy is there too, but she's graduating and begins four-year-old kindergarten this fall. So we think of this as their "first" school. Their "first" teacher's name is Heidi. Yolanda helps there as well, and therein lay some confusion. The kids called her "Landa" and we couldn't figure out why.

Alex was so cute when he talked about Heidi. Fondly, warmly, he'd say, "My Heidi". It seemed he really felt attached to his first teacher. That's nice. And Yolanda? He'd say, "My Landa". That's nice too, but we were puzzled because it all seemed a bit much. Then we had a few short talks –

"Is your teacher Yolanda?"

"Yes, she's my Landa."

Similarly –

"How's Yolanda?"

"My Landa's fine."

The day before their end-of-year picnic, I told Alex –

"Do you know what? Heidi and Yolanda will be there."

"MY LANDA COMING?"

Your Heidi, my Heidi – Yolanda, my Landa. He didn't hear "Yolanda", he heard "Your Landa", and it was a very short step to "My Landa" and "My Heidi". This is cool. We're not confused anymore.

Conversations with a four-year-old

Amy certainly has done her share to impress upon us that names are special. One evening, she was snuggling with her mom who said –

"You're my snuggle bunny."

Not one to stand by while others initiate names or ideas about her small universe, Amy said –

"No, I'm your snuggle *runny*."

When Kristen heard what Amy said, she liked the idea and used it for her school art project. It became a special name right away. Care to snuggle with Snuggle Runny? Probably not. Snuggle Runny was a tree made of paper-maché!

Amy asked me once –

"Guess what my name is? You can say for real what it is."

"Amy."

"Wrong."

"What is it?"

"Monkey."

I like it – Monkey Elizabeth Cook. It suits.

On goes the name-calling. When she's done with this one, she can pass it along to her brother because it suits him even more. What a monkey he is.

Alex and the mom

The preschool picnic around the middle of June was a fine time. There were hot dogs and drinks, chips and cake, lots of parents, lots of noise, and a mess of little kids. It was lots of fun.

It was a Friday, and afterwards we went straight to the cottage for the weekend. Anne and Andrew and their two children were coming for a visit the next day, and there's more room there, indoors and out. What's more, the warming sun that brought out the tulips in May was heating the lake at the same time. Summer was coming. We talked about that, and how we might enjoy our first swim of the year.

When our friends arrived the next morning, another beautiful day was well underway and sure enough, down we went and into the lake. The kids were excited, especially Alex with his brand new red and green water wings. He was very happy. But the water was chilly, we all were hungry, so it wasn't long before we headed back up.

Along the way, Anne said something surprising and I asked her –

"Why did you call Alex 'the kid'?"

She had a really good answer –

"Because he called me 'the mom'."

Oops. We'd carefully prepared him for a visit by six-year-old Michael and four-year-old Becky, but we forgot Mom and Dad.

We fixed that, and for the rest of their visit, here's what we heard from Alex: "Anne and AnDREW". He loved saying, "Anne and AnDREW". His emphasis on the "DREW" suggested he didn't understand why the dad had to have this extra noise tagged on at the end of his name. The mom didn't. But if he had to abide by that, he would, and everyone would know he was doing it just as he should. That's okay, it hasn't been three years since the young lad began studying English, and the first year or so was pretty much a washout.

Names and little kids, there sure is fun to be had here. With the younger ones, there often is aural confusion. Alex was cute talking about his Landa and AnDREW. He thought he had it right. Not quite. Of course, at his age he's a long way from reading, and what he hears is all there is. Add a few months though, confidence grows, and for Amy there was just no way for "bunny". It had to be "runny". All the words she's learning are new, what a good chance to toss in a few of her own.

Add a few years. Twenty or thirty would do. What do you think kids, one of your own? Maybe. Come back with one of your own. You will have been there, but not for a very long time. Now you'll be at the other end of the coupling – yours will be the big hand. Come back and listen closely, it's so beautiful. So many names, so much humour and surprise, and you'll owe it all to your little one, your very own little kid. There'll be a new name for me too: "Granddad"! And more two-year-olds, I can hardly wait.

*   *   *   *   *

They even have names for their games. After dinner one night, Amy and Lynn were going shopping. Alex wanted to go too, but it was late for him, and I suggested we could play some games instead. He liked that. First though, I turned my attention to helping Amy with her socks and shoes. She wanted to know which shoe was for which foot.

Daddy's wacko! That's okay, I'm allowed.

Teaching a little kid "left" and "right" is easy. Once the terms have been introduced, subsequent questions likely will be only about one of them, so you respond with words of explanation that are relative to the other. For instance, Alex called me once from another room, asking –

"What foot is the right foot again?"

Hmm.

"Actually, that's easy Alex. It's the one where your big toe is on the left."

This falls under the heading of "conceptual confusion" and the kids are no match for a muddleheaded dad.

Yes, it's true – Daddy's wacko. It's quite justifiable. It comes from hanging around these little ones for a long time. It's not something to find discouraging, think of it as an entitlement. Forgiving yourself should not be a problem.

It's not an all-the-time thing and it surfaces irregularly. Sometimes it's fatigue-induced, you can't do much about that. Sometimes it's sheer excitement: "HEY! I'M A DAD!" Other times, it's due to learning taking far longer than expected. It took eons for my little girl to name colours, now it seems much the same for my young boy's toilet training. Then there's the inexperience factor. When you first start out, you haven't experienced the sort of behaviour that little kids are apt to present.

One day my little kid Alex presented me with something that I thought was quite mature. Was I in for a surprise. He had found an old rattle that he hadn't seen for some time, and quickly made the association that rattles are for babies. Right on! Then he said –

"I'm going to play with this when me be a baby again. Could I?"

There are many little things that can set you off on a muddleheadedness bend. When you see your child talking on the phone and answering questions not with "Yes" or "No", but by nodding – moving that cute little round thing atop shoulders up and down or side to side – that's one of them. When your kid goes into a far-off room to get something from a dresser and hollers back, "Which drawer is it in, this one?" That's another. Then just when you think there's some understanding, you hear, "Is this my other shoe?", you reply, "Yes", and then you hear, "Is this my other shoe too?" Another. With only a small amount of applied muddleheadedness, one is able to respond in kind.

So if I tell Alex his right foot has a big toe on the left side, maybe I'm tired. Maybe I'd just watched him nodding on the phone. Maybe I'll do better next time.

Conversations with a four-year-old

Amy, Mom's ready, where are your socks and shoes?
Amy knew where, and I sat down on the floor with her.
She had her socks on in no time. I picked up a shoe –

"First you put this one on the right foot. Okay?"

"Okay."

"Then you put this other one on the left foot, do
    you know why?"

"Why?"

"Because it's the only one that's left, right?
    Amy? Do you understand me? AMY?"

Amy didn't understand me. Off they went. Was I being goofy because I was tired? Maybe. More likely, I was just having some fun with my little girl. Needless to say, she paid me no attention at all. Mom, we sure are having quite a time with these two, aren't we. Alex and I can play some games now.

*   *   *   *   *

Probably not for long though. He has a dozy look on his sweet face and soon I'll be tucking him in. A kiss, a hug, likely right to sleep and I'll be alone. Oh well, I'm tired. I might turn in too. But Amy will be home in awhile, I can look forward to seeing her to bed too. Beautiful moments at the end of a day.

Games with Alex and Amy

They were hardly out the door when he asked me –

"Can we play the elevator game?"

I lay down on my back, he lay on top, and with my hands most of the way around his waist, I lifted him up slowly with his happy face right over mine. "Going up, hats and toques", and once my arms were outstretched, down we went – "Going down, socks and boots". Just before we reached the bottom it was "Love stop", and I pulled him down and squeezed him and kissed him and wouldn't let the little daddy-climber get away even for a moment until I was finished. He laughed and squealed all the time. It was delightful.

Amy and Alex are both daddy-climbers. Mommy-climbers too, but I'm a dad and let me tell you, they climb all over me a lot. He wanted to play the airplane game, and with my hands around his waist again, up and down and around he went. When we finished that, one more –

"Now can we play the walk-on-Daddy's-face game? Could I? Hold my hands so I won't fall Daddy."

Conversations with a four-year-old

When the other two arrived home, Alex was asleep, and I wasn't far behind. Amy was though, and when my turn came to lie down with her, she was still full of it, still rarin' to go. It was very clear that my usual words – did you have fun today, that's nice, Daddy's tired, have a good sleep, would you like a goodnight kiss, and no-it's-too-late-to-read-a-book – would never do. I asked her –

"Did you buy anything at the store?"

"Yes."

"What did you buy?"

"Pee pee."

"Pee pee?"

"Yes."

I paused. Actually, there was a pause after most of Amy's turns in this conversation. Each time, it took a moment to catch what she had just said, and then figure out what to ask her next. Amy was grinning from beginning to end –

"Where is it?"

"In Mommy's drawer."

"What colour is it?"

"Orange."

"How much did it cost?"

"Forty-one pounds."

"What do you mean, forty-one pounds?"

"That's what I weigh."

"No, you only weigh thirty-one pounds."

"That's what I said. Thirty-one. Ask me another question Daddy, and I'll answer you."

"What are you going to do with it?"

"Mud. Ask me another question and I'll answer you."

Mud? Our conversation went on a little longer, but only a little, and never became any less inane. It ended when I couldn't think of more questions about thirty-one pounds of orange pee pee in Mommy's drawer. It's probably puddled up beside her Kleenex.

This was very much a game as well, an "Amy game", and every bit as dangerous as Alex's. His game sets a precedent for weight lifting, or doing bench presses with one's nose and cheek. Amy's sets a precedent for nonsense. No it doesn't. It follows a precedent set long ago. Of course, it suits Amy very well because she can play and stay awake a little longer yet, and it's already past her bedtime.

I knew that – away past her bedtime. Amy knew that too. No more questions and it took only a moment to coax her to lie down and close her eyes to sleep. Goodnight Amy, my muddy little girl. Sweet dreams.

- 5 -

Bedtime at the end of a day is extraordinary. A child's sleep is so quiet and peaceful and it's about to happen. The little one is about to begin to recharge so as to be ready to meet you in the morning. And for you, release is imminent – release from the chatter and commotion, the games and the clutter – and welcome it is, as fatigue and your adult longings play against each other for a short while before you succumb yourself.

But first, there are matters that need to be attended to. One more diaper change perhaps, pajamas, tooth brushing if there are any, and special little conversations. Several hours will go by, after all, before the two of you are together again, and a little mind strains to see that all important things have been talked about – special little talks as these matters, too, are dealt with. Soon there will be no more energy, but nothing important left either. Until that moment, you might have trouble staying away from your little one's bedroom.

The on-going awakedness is nothing more than a natural expression of enjoyment of life. And you – Mom, or you – Dad, know and feel that this is almost the same thing as enjoyment of you. Is this fun or exasperating? It's your choice. And you choose night after night, trying to balance your weariness with the beautiful moment at hand, rationalizing that your child's sleep matters. One can not escape the ambiguity of this very special time.

*   *   *   *   *

It's June now, and it's hardly been a month since we finally put away Alex's crib. He likes the new arrangement. The dark blue quilt goes well with the light blue walls. His bed is in a corner with the head of it against a wall, and the far side about a foot away from another. There's just enough room for Alex to help make his bed in the morning, or to hide in the afternoon when playing a game with his sister.

We put a guardrail on each side. They don't quite extend the entire length of his bed, so there is about a foot up by his pillow where there is no rail. Can't corner Alex – if Amy comes up the side along the wall, he can climb up through that opening onto his bed and away he goes. Of course if she comes across the bed trying to catch him, he'll just hop down through the same hole, scoot along to the foot, and scamper out the door.

He first slept in his bed in January, but only for one night. Here's why. Alex has a toy vacuum cleaner. When he pushes it, the wheels go around and stir up a bunch of plastic beads that bounce around in the top of the vacuum making all sorts of noise.

Well, he decided to vacuum the rug in our bedroom that night, and in he came. Back and forth and the beads were bouncing like crazy. What a racket! More noise as he banged into the dresser. "Alex what are you doing!" More noise as he knocked over a waste basket. We woke up quickly. IT WAS FOUR O'CLOCK IN THE MORNING! Alex was housecleaning in the dark at four in the morning, oblivious to Dad and Mom who were sound asleep a moment earlier. We turned on a light, and with a few words, put him back in bed, and the next night, back into his crib for a few more weeks, thankful we hadn't put it away yet.

We learned a lesson about cribs that night. The bars aren't there just to keep an infant from rolling out. Alex, the toddler, had ignored his parole requirements so back he went. As for his sleepy parents, we were a little optimistic in assessing his intentions, weren't we. I suspect that's natural. We felt a longing around this time to turn his nursery into a child's bedroom, to make the furniture arrangement look more lasting. Maybe at a less conscious level, there were hopeful musings that associated "crib to bed" with "diapers to underpants" or some such. Fat chance of that.

Someone's knocking at the door

So now he's in his bed and the crib is gone. The bars have been replaced by a door, and he's learning more every day about the relationship the door has with his room. It's never closed all the way, and for the most part, he respects our wishes and the time of night with all sorts of maturity. Other times he's still a little kid.

"But the light was on so I could go out."

– he said one time when we asked him what he was doing in our room. We told him we weren't home. He turned around without another word and went straight back to bed.

Usually, we would close his door most of the way, leaving it open just a crack. This would often follow a far-too-long discussion about how big the crack should be. Then awhile later, we'd sometimes hear knock, knock, knock, knock. Sure enough, Alex would be knocking at his partly open door, wanting to come out.

"What do you think Mom, should we go see who's at the door?"

"No Dad. It's late. Maybe he'll go away."

Knock, knock, knock. Alex was patient. He'd knock quietly for awhile. He wanted someone to come and open his door to the rest of the house for him. He just wasn't ready to quit yet. One time, I said to him after this had gone on some –

"Alex if you don't behave, I'm going to close your door all the way!"

With much hope and exuberance, his next words were –

"With me out?"

From somewhere else in the house, there was a voice –

"NO WITH YOU IN!"

Amy had been listening all the while.

Conversations with a four-year-old

Amy watched Alex's bedtime behaviour closely because she had her own charges with whom to deal, and she wanted to get it right. Her doll Erin – two years old, just like Alex – certainly had it right.

"Daddy, guess what."

"What?"

"Erin's only two. Sometimes, I put her in a crib. Sometimes I put her in a bed and guess what. When Erin goes to sleep in her bed she don't get out because she's a little girl. When I see her in the morning, SHE'S STILL IN BED."

There were times, though, when morning would come, and Alex would be sound asleep between Lynn and me in our big bed. Or on the other side of Lynn if Amy already had that spot. That's okay, some of the time anyway. It's all part of enjoying the kids as much as one possibly can in these early, magic years.

There were other times when morning would come.

"Can you wake up now? Can you?"

Too late, I just did. Thanks. He's no angel. Alex doesn't preface his remarks in any way to be sure he has your attention. He assumes he has it all the time. This is closer to the truth than one would like to admit, though when we're asleep might be an exception.

Another time, the first words of the day to be spoken were addressed to mother, with love, from Alex –

"Mommy, where is the lipstick Aunt Laurie gave me?"

It was Sunday, 6:36 AM. He was standing right beside the clock on the bedside table. This is different than bedtime. Here, he disturbs your rest by coming into your room rather than calling you to come into his. How considerate. Awhile later, I was out of bed and met him in the living room where he informed me –

"You were taking a long time to sleep but now you're not
    because you're awake."

Awake? Thanks Alex. I was wondering about that. Twenty-four hours a day, I'm his, I belong to my little kid.

"Daddy" in the middle of the night

"Daddy."

You wake up. Or maybe you don't. You never know for sure you heard his first call. Maybe it was his second or third. Maybe it was his twentieth. Anyway, you do wake up, it would appear. You might even open your eyes and check the time on your clock radio, but only if you think the glare of the dial won't be too bright. Do you prefer 2 AM – "Wouldn't you know it, just as I was nicely asleep", 3 AM – "Rats. Right in the middle of the best sleep I've had in a long time", or 4 AM – "I guess that's it, no more sleep for me tonight"? Which do you prefer?

"Daddy."

Too bad, now you know you're not dreaming and you're going to have to do something about it.

So I climbed out of bed and headed off towards Alex's room. I stopped in his doorway. Where was he? No sign of him anywhere. I stood still and listened. Nothing. Slowly, my eyes adjusted to the ambient light, city light reflecting off clouds and falling dimly through the window. Slowly I began to see. There was his small pillow, flat in the middle at the head of his bed. But no Alex. An inch lower on each side lay his sheet, flat on the mattress reaching evenly to the bedsides. Still no Alex. But an inch lower still, flat again, in the corner – in the hole at the end of the guardrail – soles of two little feet. I could barely make them out in the darkness.

I smiled. There's Alex – bare foot-bottoms in the corner. Kneeling on his bed, I reached over the edge and lifted up those few pounds of boy and lay them down right where they're supposed to go. He was only a bit awake. I pulled his sheet up over him and kissed his forehead and retreated quietly. In another three or four hours, getting out of bed would be more appropriate, and I hoped the little one in the next room would keep that in mind too and soon we both were sound asleep again.

PART 2

SUMMER FUN AT THE COTTAGE

- 6 -

School's out. It's late June, this time school's out for real. It has nothing to do with fire alarms. Preschool is out too. They both love school, but were they ever excited about summer holidays! Dad and Mom must have had something to do with that. A 12-year-old school / holiday mentality injected into the minds of little kids – shame on us. But they'd soon be with their good friends Lindsay and Kaitlyn for another summer, every day for two full months. All we had to do was pack the car a little more than usual and drive north, and we'd be doing that Friday after work. They could hardly wait.

It's a foursome. Lindsay was born first, three months later came Amy, then Alex, and then Kaitlyn who turned two just a couple of weeks ago. They've known one another since their beginnings. Their friends' mother's name is Joy. When we're not at the cottage, Joy will sometimes phone us during the week, or the other way around, and we'll encourage the kids to have a chat too. That's all one needs to know to understand – or perhaps "follow" is a better word – what happened one evening. This is hard to understand, and I think even Amy and Alex would agree. Fun though. It was just before we moved to the cottage.

We had company that night. Madzy was over and we were all crowded around the kitchen table. Lynn asked –

"Amy, do you want to call Joy tonight?"

"Yes."

"How about you Alex?"

"Yeah."

"Yes" and "Yeah" but really, they were way more excited than that.

"Okay. We'll do that later."

Later? The kids didn't want to do that later. They wanted to do that now. Amy said –

"Alex. Do you want to call Joy?"

"Yeah."

There was no doubt, they really wanted to do that now. So they did –

"Joy! JOY!! **JO-OY!!!!**"

A couple more times too, they called as loud as they could. Then they laughed and laughed – that was a good joke. Lynn wondered –

"Do you think Joy heard you?"

"No she live too far away."

– replied Alex.

This was so much fun that the next day he called "Joy" again as loud as he could. Only this time, he was talking to her on the telephone. This time she heard him. She's had a little difficulty hearing since, with one ear anyway, but we understand she's getting better.

Off we went on Friday. It was past nightfall before we were underway, and a few minutes later we were in the country as the city streetlights ended abruptly. "Who turned on the dark?", Alex wanted to know. I thought about how to answer him but when I turned around to say something, it didn't matter anymore. Sound asleep, both of them. All eyes closed in the back seat. No more noise from the sleeper car.

Chug, chug, chug, chug, chug....quietly into the dark night, our train chugged down the track....chug, chug, chug. Our summer fun had begun.

*   *   *   *   *

Summertime was beautiful that year. I remember it well, it was only two years ago. The ambivalence that greeted us each night at bedtime cropped up in many ways as the weeks went by. Shyness was one of those ways. Amy was shy but not Alex, and we enjoyed both ends of that continuum throughout the summer. Alex's toilet training was another. How could anyone so small and adorable make such a mess! His doll was much better behaved. Alex loved Blacks Eyes so much and he tended to her every day. But on the other hand, Amy never did attach herself similarly – more ambivalence. And it all nested in that larger ambivalence that greets a new parent whose days already are chockfull of other life dimensions. Move over everything, make room for another. It was a wonderful summer.

We moved to the cottage. Joy's family lives just up the hill, near enough that Amy and Lindsay became fast friends as the days and weeks passed by, four-year-olds both. Kaitlyn, barely two, learned her first four words: "Wait for me guys." She learned them really well. She has a booming voice and we heard them all summer long. Underpants were big in early July, they were an issue on several occasions. On one of these, we laughed so hard at Alex that I'll never forget it. Later in July, we drove to Tweed – there on Monday, back Friday, five days that were very busy and very fun. Towards the end of our trip, a little nostalgia crept in....and then out almost right away. Little kids have no patience for nostalgia, they have enough trouble with the here and now. Conceptual confusion was rampant. "Learning" was an every-day activity, and there was bound to be confusion along the way. Much of the learning came from efforts of little ones to be just like mom and dad. Is that good? So young, yet my how they wanted to grow up so fast. And by the time we moved back to the city in August, learning how not to get along with a sibling was well underway.

We moved to the cottage and into another season. The days were warmer, the lake closer, but that's not what this is about. That only shapes the playground. The game is the same and it is this. A little one – early learning, first words, and with them, a parent's first glimpse into what's on a child's mind. It happens. A little one – Amy, Alex, you, me: the universal child. It happens everywhere all the time, it always has. A little one – a two-year-old said one thing, a four-year-old used more words and said another. It happened in Ottawa and at a cottage too, it happened two years ago in the spring and summer months. What happened, what is it that happened?

Only the ordinary. A dog kissed him, it didn't bite him at all. Snow melted and a little girl wondered. One dropped a rattle on the floor, the other a butter dish, a boy started talking and called his doll "Kiki" one day. A girl had a favourite song. We put away a crib. Ordinary. It became special only when someone stopped and noticed. And then accepted. And then enjoyed, one can hardly do otherwise. And then it became magic!

Yes, we moved to the cottage in June that summer, one Friday late in the month after the dark was turned on. A different playground, but all else was the same. Alex's crib was gone from his bedroom there too, we'd dismantled it when Anne and Andrew visited. Here's another vignette about life once out of a crib –

✳   ✳   ✳   ✳   ✳

More special moments at bedtime

When the crib comes down, restraint isn't the only new issue. There's another. It's not likely that either you or your toddler, still in a crib at night, ever gave much thought to the idea of your lying down alongside. I can close my eyes and imagine myself climbing carefully over the side of his crib and squeezing in beside – not on top, beside – the little boy who asked me sweetly to lie down with him. "Move over Alex. Farther. Farther still. Oh. That's it?" No, it never came up when the crib was standing.

Now he has his own bed and it comes up all the time. Lynn and I encourage this because we love to lie down with each of them for a few words, a hug, a goodnight kiss. But then it comes up again, and sometimes – even again. It can be fun – again and even again – but there's a book or a TV show that won't be looked at, or a phone call that won't be made. There's an entirely new consideration here, we call it "callbacks".

It's a polite word. "Stalling" might be more to the point, but we try not to think of it that way. The little one wants only to prolong a liaison, and we've learned to try not to let our tiredness keep us from seeing the humour and warmth in the effort. Never does creativity blossom more than when a little mind is put to the challenge.

After brushing his teeth last night, Alex was all set for bed. Or so it seemed. Then he picked up the cup by the sink and said –

"First me need to wet this."

"No you don't, come on, let's go to bed."

"Then me need to dry it."

What a good listener – very selective. He heard "No you don't." He didn't hear "let's go to bed" at all. And if I say "No you don't", that must mean that it's already wet. So of course he has to dry it. Very logical. The logic may be incomplete, but it's just fine from a two-year-old's viewpoint. He doesn't really know what he wants; but it's not to be left alone, close his eyes, and go to sleep. That's what I want, not him. So I could pass him a towel, talk about something else if I thought he'd listen, or become a little stern or impatient with his gambit. With this latter option though, you need to be careful or you might miss something.

One night after several callbacks, Lynn and I were both leaning towards stern. Then once again –

"Mommy."

"WHAT!"

With a barely audible voice, he said –

"I love you."

You wouldn't want to miss that. Beautiful. Just a short while later –

"Mommy, me want cold water."

"Yes dear, I'll get you some right away."

So he tells his mother he loves her, softens her right up, and then calls room service whenever he feels like it. It could go on for awhile, couldn't it, and then it would be time for another "WHAT!" / "I love you." It's hard to be upset. I know. There have been other times when he's done the same to me.

"Daddy."

"You go to sleep Alex."

"But guess what?"

"WHAT!"

Back came that same soft, warm answer that makes one feel just terrible for raising one's voice. I went to his room and stood in the doorway. Very humbly, I said –

"I love you too Alex. Good night boy."

And I walked away thinking –

> So what if his "I love you" was defensive. It was beautiful.
> Why did he have to be defensive? Why was I impatient?
> He's only two years old! Was it a game? If I had said
> "what?" instead of "WHAT!", what would he have said?
> I'll never know. It wasn't a game, it was beautiful. Magic
> years. Such a reluctance to close his eyes to the two people
> he loves the most.

It's hard to be upset. You might be called back for another hug and a kiss, or maybe to be told quite accurately that the two of you forgot to rub noses. Indeed, you may well put aside your weariness and go back to his room without his call. You might see him holding Blacks Eyes up high by the window so she can see the moon. You might find him reading one of his favourite books in the dark. Too dark for me to read, but if all you're interested in are the pictures and you've seen them many times before when there was ample light, then a dark, little-distinguished outline is all that you really need. You might go back and have a quiet little talk like this –

"Mommy, where did I get this pillow?"

"I made it for you when you were a little baby."

"Oh thank you. Thank you for making it for me."

"I made it for you because I loved you a lot."

"Oh thank you for loving me Mommy."

So special. Words like these just melt your tiredness into a puddle of warmth and good feeling about your child. And about yourself too. And about the growing love the two of you share.

* * * * *

Amy knows how to stall too. In fact, she is Alex's mentor, although he's taken it all a step further. Amy's approach at the moment is to make one last trip to the potty, even though it's not necessary. Then she'll wait for Lynn or I to come and talk to her. Just what she says will depend on what she remembers having happened lately that she thinks might be appropriate: a bit amusing, so maybe Mom or Dad won't be annoyed with this tactic. For instance, "My pee pee's still in Ottawa." Amy's stalling is worldly. "My pee pee went to New York."

There are several variations – "My pee pee's having lunch", "My pee pee's stuck in traffic", "My pee pee's having a nap." They're all reasons why her trip to the bathroom isn't about pee pee at all.

Conversations with a four-year-old

One night, I lay down with Amy and her doll Erin. Amy had been playing a lot with her that day. She said –

> "Guess what. Erin loves broccoli. I gave her one bite and then she finished it all. Because she loved it. And guess what she said?"

> "Thank you."

Amy paused for a long time. She was thinking. I took the words right out of her mouth, didn't I; she'd have to come up with something else. Here's what she came up with –

> "No. She said, 'You're welcome for giving me that and could you give me some more tomorrow?' "

She could. But she didn't, no broccoli for Erin the next day. After supper that evening though, Amy said she had something special to tell me. It was bedtime again. I told her she could lie down in our room, and when she fell asleep I'd carry her into her room. Nothing new here – she often asked if she could do this. This time though, I offered first because I wanted to hear what was on her mind, so upstairs we went. And we lay down in our room.

> "If the other people say the other words that I
> was going to say, that means me say, 'Hey.
> I was going to say that'."

She laughed and we chatted for awhile about all of this. And when she fell asleep I carried her into her room.

Later on, I went back and kissed her gently. I love her so much.

Then there's Blacks Eyes. She helps Alex stall, but that's what friends are for. She does this by adding a step to the small ritual that transpires when I'm about to lie down with him. You see, there's only so much room. Alex lies down on one side of his bed, and on the other side is another small pillow. Who gets it, Blacks Eyes or me? Deciding this is the added step.

You don't always know who the authority is here. One would expect it to be Alex, and usually it is. One night he said –

"I don't want Blacks Eyes to have her pillow. You can have it."

"No, we'll share it, and when I go, she can have the whole thing."

"And when Mommy goes, she can have the other whole thing."

Yes she can – both whole things. Thanks Alex, and I lay down. The very next night the question came up again. This time he yielded to his little friend –

"Blacks Eyes, can Daddy lay on your pillow?"

He turned to me and said –

"I heard. She said 'yes'."

I lay down again. What a good doll.

Alex and Blacks Eyes

Lynn and I often noticed how wide was the gulf between our two children regarding feelings towards a particular toy. Amy's interest would never extend more than a week or two, while Alex's affection for his doll went on and on. That's the way it was going to be and that's all there was to it.

"I'm her dad. Always. ALWAYS! Always I said. Always."

– explained Alex one day.

We didn't have two children, we had three: Amy, Alex, and then Blacks Eyes was born. We never would have thought of "Blacks Eyes" as a name for a third child, but then it wasn't our choice. Her demands for attention were significant and it seems we did our best to meet them. I must have a dozen pictures of our little boy lying in his bed sound asleep with his arm tight around Blacks Eyes. Occasionally there would be a variation – a small plastic frog sitting on top of her, or something like that. Usually, it was just him and her and I couldn't leave my camera alone.

They were inseparable, and – should we be concerned? What if she broke? We discussed this with Alex, and he knew how to say –

"I have to hang on to Blacks Eyes carefully because she's
    breakable."

What if he lost her? There were a few "What ifs", and we sometimes wondered if his attachment was too strong. We wondered if he'd be too upset if something happened. We wondered.

One morning not long ago, Alex had just awakened and when I sat down on the side of his bed, he asked me right away where was Blacks Eyes. I said –

"She's not far away, here she is. She just fell off the bed."

"Well if we threw her she'd be far away."

We wondered. But never very long. No, we're not worried about Alex and his doll. Moreover, if he wants to brag about being her dad, that's all right too. In fact that's just excellent because it hasn't always been that way. Amy and Alex had a brief chat the other day. Alex was hugging Blacks Eyes, and he said to Amy –

"When I grow up, I'm going to be a daddy."

"When I grow up, I'm going to be a mommy."

"Well I'm already Blacks Eyes' mommy."

It was very brief. Alex stood up and left the room. Blacks Eyes left too.

Conversations with a four-year-old

So off they went, as Amy completely ignored his pretense to motherhood. I sat down right away. I wanted to talk to her and hear what she had to say about being a mother herself. Now was my chance, I could catch up to the other two later.

Our conversation, though it rambled, reflected a good amount of conceptual learning. There are still some gaps but their days are numbered. And I wrote it all down. Amy continued –

"I am. I play 'Babies' and they sleep a lot. They eat breakfast and I feed them."

"Do they go to the potty?"

"Only a baby potty."

"Do they cry a lot?"

"No. But they play a lot."

"What do they play?"

"They play 'Crawl, baby, crawl'."

"How do you play that?"

"You crawl and see who the winner is. And they drink milk a lot. Okay?"

"What else do they do?"

"They eat a lot. Now they're pretty strong. Well Adriana, do you know how old she is? She's six."

"What do they eat?"

"They eat a lot of baby food except Adriana. She eats big girl food."

"What's her favourite?"

"Spaghetti. That's my favourite, that's why I said it."

"How many babies do you have?"

"I only have three. Two babies and one big girl. No, three babies. I have Aunt Sylvia and Erin and the one that Kinnon gave me. I never named her. Her name is Julie."

"I thought you said you never named her?"

"I just named her now."

So. Now you've met our four-year-old daughter's children: Julie, Aunt Sylvia, Erin, and six-year-old Adriana. Just call me Granddad. It sounds like Amy is well into motherhood, she understands it all. As for Alex? Well, he is Blacks Eyes' mother – nothing to scoff at there.

But he was her mother that one time only. Alex is many things to Blacks Eyes. He's her babysitter, "Blacks Eyes is a baby, so I'm babysitting." Most certainly, he's her best friend. "Guess what. Blacks Eyes is my very best friend in the wide world and NO ONE ELSE." I think he meant it. Then one day he married her. It was a tough decision, three made it to his short list: Aunt Jane, Mommy, and Blacks Eyes. Blacks Eyes got the nod.

Mostly though, he's her dad. He likes to tell me about this –

"Blacks Eyes loves her dad so much."

"Who's her dad?"

"Me. She's my baby."

He was hugging her while we talked. He once told me that's what she likes –

"Where is Blacks Eyes? Oh, there she is. Do you like when I hug her? She likes when I hug her real tight. There. She likes that."

I like that too. He's very cute when he hugs his doll.

Recently one evening, it was away past Alex's bedtime. He was in bed all right, but sleep eluded him. He was going on and on, still with a twinkle in his eye only a little bit dimmed by the hour. Amidst all his banter he gave me an opening. He said –

"I'm pretending I'm Blacks Eyes. Is that okay?"

"YES. But remember. Blacks Eyes is very quiet."

Looking right into my eyes, he closed his mouth tightly. Not a word. Then he pretended to be sleeping and closed his eyes very tightly also. Well, he never did recover from that feigned sleep. His eyes relaxed but stayed closed as the rest of him joined his game. Sleep had arrived, and another beautiful day with Alex and Blacks Eyes was over.

*   *   *   *   *

Rachel was coming to the cottage for a sleepover. She and Amy are only a few days apart in age and they've known each other all along. Amy wanted to phone and tell her she had some stickers for her. I looked up the phone number, Amy dialed, and here's most of what I heard her say while I was sitting in the next room making notes. My note-making was easy this time – the kids were oblivious. Of course, I could only hear Amy's end of the call but it didn't sound complicated, at least until Alex joined in.

"Hi Rachel. When you come for your sleepover, do you think we should be crazy?"

Then she said –

"Alex likes being crazy."

And then –

"I don't think so, let's be quiet."

And –

"I love you too, I have some stickers for you."

She handed the phone to her brother, saying –

"Alex, it's for you. It's Rachel."

Alex had a turn –

"Hi Rachel. I like to be crazy."

When Amy heard Alex say that, she said to him right away –

"Well we're not going to be crazy, tell her that."

She said that rather sternly, I thought. Here's what Alex passed along –

"Do you want to be crazy or not? No?"

"ALEX WON'T LET ME TALK TO RACHEL!"

– said Amy. And with that, Alex gave her back the phone, and she said to Rachel –

"Hello. Well, I don't know if we should be crazy or not."

So there you have it – a couple of early four-year-olds talking on the phone with interjections from a younger brother. It all seemed typical to me and I was happy to have my pencil handy.

Making notes

Making notes was an almost-all-the-time proposition. In the beginning, I tried to save it all up until the end of my children's day and then write it down. Very quickly though I became aware that it was important to note Amy's and Alex's exact words. It just didn't seem right if I forgot a few and had to improvise. This presented me with a small problem. I sometimes felt my note-making was intrusive, and that it interfered with their otherwise spontaneous play.

When Amy finished talking with Rachel, I asked her to tell me what she meant by being crazy. I wasn't about to ask Alex because I was sure he didn't know the word, even though so often his behaviour conformed so well. Amy is more apt to be quiet and gentle, and I wasn't sure how "crazy" would be appropriate. So I asked her what she meant –

"I mean by crazy when we be so excited."

"Have you been crazy with Rachel before?"

"No."

"Tell me more what you mean by 'excited'."

"I don't know more."

"When you're crazy, are you good or bad?"

"We're good."

"When Alex is crazy, is he good or bad?"

Amy thought about that one –

"He's good. But he's just funny. He looks funny."

I wrote all this down too, feeling a little guilty while so doing, but persevering nonetheless. What a little kid needs at this age is a contributor, a catalyst. You know – A DAD! What did Amy and Alex get? An historian.

Four-year-olds don't need historians. Some day, I'm going to have to apologize.

Conversations with a four-year-old

We have a new policy in our family. It was all Amy's idea. She was going out to play with her friends, and Lynn had given her some apple juice to take with her. After she returned home, Lynn asked her –

"How was your apple juice, nice and cold?"

"Yes. I couldn't find it."

"You forgot it at home, didn't you."

"Yes. But I drank it all when I got home. I'm sorry Mommy, that's all right."

She forgave herself. Isn't that a good policy? It's an especially good one to have in place for those times when no one else really wants to forgive you.

Here's an opportunity for me to try out Amy's new policy. It's one of those many inane conversations that go nowhere but are always so much fun. It was dinnertime, and Alex had an enormous dinner. This was unusual. We discussed his indulgence, with Lynn beginning –

"I think you're going to explode."

Amy then suggested –

"He might even blow down."

I wasn't quite sure what Amy meant by that, but Lynn laughed and said to me –

"I think she means 'blow up'."

Alex had an idea what she meant –

"Or maybe she means 'Pop'."

Even Amy had an idea what she meant –

"Or maybe 'Pop goes the weasel'."

I'd heard enough. Quickly, I went to get my pencil and paper. I came back and said to Alex –

"Would you like another bite?"

"Yes but I'm not going to go 'Pop goes the weasel', did you write that down?"

I wrote that down. Caught again – I'm sorry you two. That's all right.

- 8 -

Amy says "Guess what" a lot. You may have noticed. "Daddy, guess what. I have the giggles." And the other night, just before going to sleep, she was telling me all about her doll's food preferences. "Guess what. Erin loves broccoli."

From the back window of a bus in late June, she said –

"Guess what. There's a lady pushing a stroller, and there's
   another lady pushing a stroller. That's what."

Another time she told me about hot air balloons off in the distance –

"Guess what. When balloons are far away, that means they're so
   little."

Yes it does, little hot air balloons. The big ones are the ones that are close by.

Amy's "Guess what" became a habit and went on for a long time. Eventually, Lynn and I decided to do something, so guess what we did? We guessed. Of course there weren't any ground rules for her use of these words, so sometimes we guessed very slowly. Furthermore, we could hardly be faulted if as often as not our guesses were off-topic and ludicrous. Amy's reaction was predictable. First she was curious, then amused, then a little impatient, then a lot impatient, and it wasn't long before her "Guess what" turned into "Guess what. I WILL TELL YOU WHAT." And soon after that it was gone.

It still creeps back into her jargon from time to time, and if it's only occasionally, we ignore it. Otherwise, a purposefully constructed guess or two is all it ever takes to get her back on track.

Here she goes one more time –

"Guess what. I can't talk as loud as Alex. I just can't. I don't know how."

Good for you Amy, you've done well to not know how to do this.

Although Alex is the louder of the two, raising his voice is not his way of getting attention. He has a much more effective approach to this issue. If he was older, you might say it was a clever approach. He'll say –

"Daddy, do you want me to tell you this?"

And he has my attention right away. Even if I just *thought* I heard him say that, but wasn't sure, I'd still answer "Yes" right away. Wouldn't any sensible parent? You wouldn't want to say "No", and later wonder what it was that he really didn't want to tell you, but felt that he at least had to offer.

*   *   *   *   *

A word about shyness

Amy. That's the word. If I tell you more about Amy, I can tell you about shyness at the same time. It's really quite beautiful. But for Amy? Well, she'd rather not be shy if she could help it. No one likes to be self-conscious, and what's more, how can she get attention when she's shy? At home, it's easy. She just bellows "GUESS WHAT" and the job is done. If others are around though, she's more apt to deny her natural spontaneity in favour of another childish urge. She's more apt to very shyly say nothing.

Amy is shy....

Kinnon lives one cottage over in the summertime, and now and again would come by to babysit. One time when she did this a year ago, she gave Amy a doll. It never received much attention, though it's the one Amy named "Julie" right while I was talking with her. Last night, Kinnon dropped by to babysit again. Before we left, I went back to Amy's room and brought Julie out. I thought Amy would like to tell Kinnon about her new name. So I asked Amy who had given her this doll and her response was absolute shyness. Amy looked so self-conscious as she gave us a small embarrassed smile and said not a word. I hadn't seen such a sheepish presentation in a long time. Her craving for attention was entirely contradicted by shyness – what a disarming contradiction.

.. and she knows she's shy, ...

A few days before school ended and we moved to the cottage, we asked Allyson to come over to look after Amy and Alex. Lynn and I wanted to do some after-dinner shopping, but it was a little late to take the kids with us. They like Allyson, Amy was particularly excited. Allyson arrived. We heard her come in downstairs and Amy was anxious to go down to say hello. I said go ahead, but she replied –

"I want Alex to come with me because I'm kind of shy."

Alex heard her but said nothing. Amy was still anxious –

"Oh I'll go myself, I know that I'm not shy."

Silence. And then –

"Do you want to come with me Alex?"

...and she's always been shy, ...

When Amy was approaching her second birthday, my work took me out of the country for three weeks. That's a long time to be away from a two-year-old princess. I had some pictures, and that helped, but was I ever excited when my homecoming plane approached Ottawa. Mom said she'd bring Amy to the airport to meet me. Patiently I lined up at customs, waited for my suitcase to come around, and at last, headed towards the door.

I had no idea what to expect from Amy by way of a greeting. We hadn't been through this before. I thought about it before we landed, and a number of possibilities came to mind. She might –

- come running to me,
- look up and catch my eye,
- smile or grin or laugh,
- put her arms around me,
- shout something like "Daddy!",
- all of the above, or maybe,
- none of the above. Maybe she'd be asleep and I'd
  have to wake her up.

I was excited, and I was curious too.

When I went through the door, *only one* of these happened. You'll never guess which one. It was the first one on the list. She came running up to me. That's it, nothing more. She didn't touch me, and I didn't even see her. I came out the door, stopped, and looked to the left, right, and straight ahead. But not down. Gradually, I became aware that there was something right in front of me. My sub-conscience said, "This is not a good time to start walking." Then I looked down.

I saw the top of a blond head about three and a half feet below, and an inch in front of my knees. It could have been anyone who was short! Slowly, carefully, I squatted down. The second one became irrelevant, no need to look up anymore. Then, we were nose to nose. It was Amy. Then came the smile, grin, the laugh, then came the arms around me, and a little later came loud noises, "Daddy" or something, I forget, and I knew I was home. Shyness and homecomings are wonderful! And when they happen at the same time – WOW!

Last spring, I made the same trip again, and coming home I could hardly wait. My memories of that greeting I'd received two years earlier were so strong and wonderful. This time though, she was twice as old as then, what would she do this time? I came out the door. No running, no arms around me, no hug no kiss, just –

"Guess what, I love you. When you were away, Alex bit me in
the back."

Homecomings are wonderful? Did I say that?

....but can she ever embarrass you when she wants to.

Amy and Lynn were at a banking centre, Lindsay and Joy were along too. There were two machines, and seven or eight people in line waiting to use them. Not Amy though. She was being goofy, running about giggling and screaming. Lynn picked her up and said –

"Where's your mother!"

"SHE'S IN JAIL!"

Amy's reply was immediate and loud. Lynn looked around, quite embarrassed – and said, loudly enough for everyone to hear – and said, because she felt she had to – and said, not wanting to let Amy have the last word on this matter, given what Amy's last word was – and said –

"No she's not, I'm your mother."

Chalk one up for Amy. And Mom, don't you wish she was still shy? She is actually, that was an aberration.

*   *   *   *   *

Another word about shyness

The four of us were walking around the Rideau Centre one Saturday morning taking in the sights, playing little games, shopping. The Rideau Centre is a large shopping centre in the middle of Ottawa. The kids were tired and in our arms – Alex in mine, Lynn was carrying Amy – when we approached a policeman who had a handful of pamphlets regarding the police child safety program.

Amy was just the right age and the policeman took a liking to her right away. He asked her how old she was. Amy said nothing, Lynn said four. Do you go to preschool? Amy smiled, Lynn talked about her moving on up to kindergarten in the fall. Are you looking forward to kindergarten? Amy squirmed and Lynn said yes. Then he told her that a police officer would be visiting her class to talk about sidewalks and street-crossing and the like, all the while looking right into our beautiful little self-conscious daughter's eyes. Her shyness was wonderful, so much at odds with her other-times spunk. As he neared the end of his brief monologue (there was no way Amy was about to turn it into a conversation), he was loudly interrupted –

"AND I'M AMY'S BROTHER!"

The other word about shyness is "not" and that's Alex through and through.

Alex is not shy, never has been, never will be, and can be just as embarrassing as Amy can, probably more....

I can't remember Alex ever being shy. He learned to walk a couple of months after his first birthday, and about six weeks later, he had his first walking session. He loved his newfound mobility. Lynn had taken him to a shopping mall, a very long shopping mall, and he walked from one end to the other and back. He wouldn't let Lynn touch him. He'd walk up to a stranger sitting on a bench, stop in front of her or him, and – break out laughing. It was a sign of things to come.

So now he talks. He'll go into a restaurant, casually approach a table, stop, patiently wait until the diner looks up, and say, "What are you eating?" He's always approaching strangers. His most common opener is "What's your name?" but he has other questions or comments too: "Where did you get that shirt?", "I like your haircut.", "How old are you?", "When's your birthday?", he said to the lady in the elevator. He's quite a conversationalist, albeit a little weak on follow-up questions.

A mother and her 20-year-old daughter were in the next booth in a restaurant, and when the younger of the two left to get some napkins, Alex said to the mother, "What's your sister's name?" That was a very nice thing to say, wasn't it. He excelled in restaurants, but his boldness went with him everywhere.

He would be bold in his backpack, bold up high on Mom's or Dad's shoulders, bold up and then down on an escalator – fun! – very bold on the odd pony ride at a country fair. If we took the car, he used to be bold in his infant car seat, and then bold in his regular one. Then one day – no car seat. No car. And he was as bold as ever on "THE BUS! ME CAN GET UP AND WALK AROUND!" Here we go, first night out of a crib all over again.

Alex loves buses. Lots of strangers for his questions. And of course there's the big back seat. I'd hang on to him when he'd want to stand up and look out the big back window.

"Those two waved at you Alex."

"I waved back at them."

"I know, I saw you."

"I love them."

"What are their names?"

"I don't know. When I don't know their names, that means I don't love them."

He's a little philosopher, isn't he. He'll still talk to them though – again and again and again. That's Alex, not shy, outgoing, even a little cocky once in awhile.

Alex's cockiness got the better of him one day, and I was embarrassed. Sometimes it's "lack of shyness", in more extreme instances, it's "cockiness". If the trend continues, I can see other words coming into play. "Criminal" might be one of them, "just plain stupid" another. Today it was cockiness.

We'd gone to the animal hospital. I was inside, talking to someone, and I didn't twig to what was going on outside. Alex was blocking the door and saying to a very old lady, "You need to stay outside." Of course, she didn't think that was the case at all, but she was quite frail, and Alex – not quite three – seemed to have the upper hand. She'd try to slip by, he'd move over and push her and say, "You need to stay outside." I interceded as quickly as I could, and took Alex's hand and pulled him away. I said, "No she doesn't need to stay outside, she wants to come in."

And she did, but she stopped in front of us and looked down at Alex. Oh oh. Then she smiled and said, "You're cute."

Phew! So Alex is cute. That is SUCH a good thing.

Five or six years ago, if I was writing about moments of embarrassment, I'd tell you all about walking my gagawaggin' friend Scott in the park on a sunny very very muddy springtime day, and the friendly lady who greeted him, impeccably dressed in an off-white pantsuit, and how Scott greeted her, and how off-white her pantsuit was after that, and….. Enough.

Yes, you might be wondering. Who's going to embarrass you more, dogs or little kids? I should know. I used to think there was no way little kids could embarrass you the way a couple of dogs could. But then I had a couple of kids. Now I'm not so sure. I think it's a toss-up, and it probably depends on who you're with at the time.

9

Kitty

Alex and I were going shopping, we were off to the mall and we'd grab a bite to eat there as well. He looked very cute. His hair was tousled – he needed a haircut – and his face was clean, as were his clothes. I was happy to be going out with my little boy.

And he was every bit himself. So when we found ourselves beside a lady while walking hand in hand across the parking lot, he looked up at her and said –

"What's your name?"

"Kitty."

"Why is you a kitty?"

The lady smiled, and it was my turn. I explained to her that my son was only two, and….. Well, she knew that. Then she told me of another child about that age who had asked her what her name was, and when she said "Kitty", the child said –

"We got one too."

Hey! Another cute little kid, how about that. They're all over the place! In the springtime, out they come. You'll find them marching into a tulip bed, or picking dandelions along the way for dad and mom. When it's hot in the summer, all wet along a sandy beach is where you'll find them. You'll see part of them anyway, gleeful in a pile of autumn leaves, part of them peeking out from behind a snowman on a not-too-cold winter day. All year long, they're everywhere!

You might find one standing right in front of you looking up. It may even ask you a personal question: "What's your name?" or "How old are you?" or "What are you eating?" If it does, it's not rudeness, and don't think of it as an intrusion. It's just a case where you have a two-year-old in front of you. That's all.

*   *   *   *   *

Why are little kids cute? They really are you know – just look at the abundance of photographs. Just look at the little ones themselves. The first thing you see are those enormous eyes, side by side and not far apart at all. Right below is the nose. Look closely, it's very small; you never see a big one on a little kid. Sometimes at first you don't even see any hair. Before long though, it's there – silky smooth, soft, down-like, always well worth the wait. Do you have your camera ready? Cuteness is fast becoming a fact of life.

Now look closely at the skin. Often you'll see extraneous colours and bumps from the likes of tumbles, ketchup, mosquito bites, ice cream – face-painting at the fair that's been there an hour or two. These are just surface toppings, and once washed and fixed, the complexion is as soft and appealing as the rest. The underlying cuteness is restored and the facial aesthetics are complete. Take a picture. Just beautiful.

What did you get? Was it a smile? A pout? Perhaps a distressing look of sadness, or maybe a very sad look of complete fatigue. These soft appealing features work together so well that a child can screw up a face into any number of configurations; you need considerable camera memory. What's common to them all though is genuineness. You know it's for real in this early going because little kids have no guile at all.

Now close your eyes and listen. Hear the giggling, listen to the playful howling and squealing, the cackling, chortling. Some crying can be soft and gentle, listen to that too. And more giggling.

How about the occasional humming, a little tune running through a child's head while immersed in play. For certain it's something you've never heard before and neither has anyone else. Homemade and wonderful! Listen for those gleeful gales of laughter that come along daily with little prompting, if any. They're so carefree and infectious that you might find yourself laughing just as hard even though you're nowhere near as cute.

Soft aesthetics and wonderful noises catch your eyes and ears every day. What about early traveling efforts, room-to-room expeditions? To start, it might be not much more than crawling backwards, with corners and the underside of tabletops setting the boundaries. It's not long though before those first precarious steps – one two, then four or five. They're so tentative, so fun to see, so full of sudden sit-downs and smiles and pleading faces of the "Look-mommy-look-daddy-watch-me" variety. Soon it happens. Counting ceases and walking is theirs forever.

Yes, running follows, you knew it would. Did you know it would be only a day or two later? First tries at that are pure adventure: awkward, head-long dashes into furniture, knees, dogs, anything at all that lifts up a third dimension. There should be some glue on walk, something to help one stick to basics awhile. Practice is good. Maybe a speed limit would help – say a quarter of a mile per hour? Any effort at coordination is quickly abandoned in this early traveling, and this makes them cuter still.

Laughing, noisy, chubby, unkempt, jerky, and oh so cute, they stumble along. But it's just beginning. Are you ready? Quick, put away your camera! The foundation is in place, preparations are over. UNPRECEDENTED CUTENESS IS JUST AROUND THE CORNER!

*   *   *   *   *

THERE IT IS! Around the corner and under the coffee table! There's more leaning against the couch! Stand up little one, stand up and say something. Let's go! A quarter mile an hour? That's away too slow! Fireman, where are you? We need more coal. Throw it right in here, I'll hold the door. Here we go! All aboard? *How can you not hear the steam whistle!*

It seems like only a week ago when someone at the train station hollered "All aboard!" and off we went. Off to explore the humour and warmth – the laughing and the mush. Off we went to enjoy the ambience of living with a little kid. Not much winter but a lot of spring, and here we are at the cottage. Let's stop a moment. What's going on here anyway? The lady at the animal hospital thinks my little boy is cute. Alex IS cute. She was absolutely right. But then, are not all children cute when they're little kids? They sure are, why is that? Why are little kids cute?

They really are you know – they talk and they do, that's why. They use words, they never used to do that. They do more and more activities that they never used to do either. They think about all this newness too, and they respond. Their innocent expressiveness is so pervasive in the magic of early parenting. And indeed, "magic" it is. It's hard to believe that it's real; it's just so wonderful so much of the time.

It is so funny and so warm! Hand in hand, humour and warmth abound as children go about their play. They fall out of the normal events, instincts, and reactions of every child's early life. Little ones all take a turn with learning to walk, toilet training, dolls, games, names, secrets, birthdays, and so on. Then they take another turn, and another. They learn concepts bit by bit. They learn words bit by bit by bit. Some words are basic, essential – "no" and "why" for instance. Some are special like "Mommy" and "Daddy" and "I love you". And with no doubt, there are words that make no sense at all when they're first used. This is very fun though, and just fine if you're a beginner. Bit by bit, it does take a little time.

The learning proceeds slowly and deliberately as all the while, other things interfere. Sleep, a bottle, a crying spell, a new sibling, a new season, but then, there really is no hurry. Little kids have superb memories that let the layering-on go forward at not too quick a pace. Parents choose the slow route and this is understandable. The special magic will fade far too soon as it is, dragging one's feet is okay.

All of this learning comes face to face with the little-kid personality. With just a year or two of life so far, uncluttered minds provide little preconception, and freshness of response is to be expected. It's delivered regularly – imaginations are strong. Wanting to impress is even stronger. Curiosity is an imperative. There's an enormous craving for attention, but sometimes it runs head-on into shyness. Sometimes one sees sudden bursts of wide-eyed enthusiasm, other times a quiet turning-in for no apparent reason. Misconceptions, contradictions, ambiguities are frequent, and an observant eye and an attentive ear are in for a real treat. The days are full of surprises. As a result, one laughs a lot, and there are oohs and aahs and goose bumps and tears and warm feelings all over.

It's this mixing of staggered learning with a personality just beginning that is largely behind this cuteness. Children are introduced to a word in one context but they turn around and with much gusto, use it in another. You can understand why the child might choose to use it in this varying context, but really, it's not quite right and something else would have done better. Similarly, when they eagerly show you their mastery of basic concepts, as often as not it falls short. All they really show you is a smattering of partial learning. Their expression will be different once they're further along, but until then, the ensuing cuteness is nothing short of magic.

Here's an example. What might have been said when you had your first little talk about the moon? Not much, not very many words. Likely it was bright eyes, a little noise, a little finger pointing upwards, and you replied softly, "That's the moon sweetheart. Isn't it pretty?" Not much more than a visual object-recognition exercise. So what could you expect another time when you're outside and the moon is high and bright in the sky? You really have no idea. Here's what Alex said one night when we opened the door and went out –

"The moon! Look! We got one of them at the cottage!"

Now isn't that funny? This is a good example. Only a two-year-old can look up and say this. A one-year-old doesn't know the words, a three-year-old would find the notion of more moons absurd. So you reply, "Yes, and I think I saw one at Grandpa's the other night too", and get on with it. But you smile, and think to yourself what a funny thing my little boy just said. And you feel really good about your early-parenting experience.

Humour and warmth. Every day, the warmth comes at you all by itself. Just a glance will do it. Often though, it follows the humour directly and this is so endearing. You laugh so hard at something your little one says and your laughter, being such a strong emotion, leads you to look closely at its source: your son. Or your little daughter. That's who made you laugh so hard. Yours. And you feel unbelievably warm. This happens regularly during these magical, first few years.

It's the unordered, and – for such a long time – incomplete, ad hoc presentation of words and concepts. Mix in some shyness and imagination. Consider the history of unrestrained expressiveness. Then there's the void of preconception. Add a cute face. Put all of this together and it's humour and warmth all the time. Especially when the self-expression is directed towards an adult, educated set of ears and eyes. Especially when it's bounced off a perspective that is complete enough, likely right, and likely unchanged for years. The freshness is wonderful, the expectation absolutely non-existent, the emotion so very, very fulfilling. And your child? Yes – *your* child?

Your child is special, incredibly so, and there are times when you wish your days together could stay the same forever.

> Listen to the steam whistle! See the vapour pluming into the summer sky. Hear the little ones. What excitement! Are you ready? *How can you not be ready!* **ALL ABOARD!!!**

*   *   *   *   *

So off we go again, looking for more laughing and mush. Little kids sure are cute. They show you that right from the very beginning. And when they start to talk, every day they tell you that too.

> *Conversations, such as they are, with a one-year-old*
>
> When Amy was about fourteen months, there was a very singular incident that taught me suddenly and thoroughly just how delightful a child's innocence can be. It happened in the bathtub.

She was at that brief age when she'd learned a little about a few words, but not nearly enough to take them and use them properly in different contexts. But she really wanted to do that.

She knew how to say "bye bye" when I went to work. She was beginning to know what "no" meant, she'd certainly heard it enough. Did she know what "love" meant? Of course not, but try to tell her that.

She was having a bath, I was standing beside the tub, and I said –

"Amy, do you love me?"

"No."

Her tone suggested she wasn't sure that this was the right answer at all. I paused, and then looking a little sad, and lingering on the word "like", I said –

"Do you like me?"

"No, no….. No."

She shook her head from side to side this time, but it was very clear that her tone of unsureness about how her answer might sit with me was now one of concern. Still sadder, I said –

"Do you miss me when I go to work?"

Her face lit up. With bright eyes, a big smile, and ever so much warmth – and relief – she looked up at me and happily said –

"Bye bye."

Amy's words, her limited understanding of them, her genuine feeling about them, and about me too, all came together for a moment. It was overwhelming.

….and rocket candies. I knew nothing about "rocket candies" until I knew Alex. Now, at least in our small family context, the words are unforgettable. It began on Halloween with Alex being a bit over a year old. We dressed him up as a pumpkin and carried him from door to door so he could do his trick-or-treating. Lots of rocket candies went into his bag, far too many for him to eat at his young age. So we put them aside, and a year later they were to become the first sop in our early efforts to persuade Alex to acknowledge that indeed, there is some merit in toilet training.

They have a tart, fruity taste and they're good. Alex loves them, so it seemed like an excellent idea to use them as we did. If we could control the dispensing of them, we might succeed in gaining his confidence about the status of his bladder, and so on. Quickly taking off a clean diaper is very pleasurable when you think about the alternative, and a little warning from our little boy would be nice.

He had his first rocket candy last January. It was time. It was a momentous occasion, our first small step towards that mighty, elusive goal: *Underpants*! We'd give him one if he had a successful trip to the potty, we'd call it "tinkle tinkle". We'd give him two if there was a "kerplunk". Often he'd call them "candy pills". That was easier for him to say, and soon we heard that almost all the time. He had one other name for them too that would surface now and then.

Here's a riddle: What do you call two rocket candies held tightly together with your thumb and first finger? A "Frosty". Okay, so it's not really a snowman. But if your two-and-a-half year old toddler, not yet toilet trained, says it's a Frosty, you say, "Eat him quick before he melts." Alex's favourite movie back then was "Frosty the Snowman", and I remember so well the first time he watched it.

One big tear

It was five o'clock one cold winter morning. Alex woke up and couldn't go back to sleep so we went to the living room. He sat down on the middle of the floor while I turned on the television. We'd just bought it the night before, and I thought I could return to bed for awhile because Alex would enjoy it. It certainly is for little ones. Frosty is the hero, and he behaves like one for most of the story until he finds himself in a jam and melts into a puddle. Poor Frosty. Well I couldn't go back to sleep either and I came out to join Alex. Quietly, I walked down the hall and when I saw his face, wide-eyed and totally intent on the movie, I stopped.

There are tears and there are tears – with a couple of little ones like our two, you're going to see them all. But I'd never seen a tear as big as the one slowly sliding down Alex's cheek, glistening in the light of the television set, the only light at that hour of the winter morn. One wouldn't think Frosty the Snowman could do this, could draw out such an enormous tear. It did though, and for a moment my son was a very little boy with a big, big heart.

It was a beautiful moment, and I shared it with the girls downstairs. Lauren was in the basement when I went down with a load of laundry. A while later I left for work and dropped in at Jane's daycare to say goodbye to Amy and Alex. Picture this.

Alex was parked right in front of the television. Frosty was playing of course. All around him were Kelly, Kristen, and Lauren – Amy too. I heard some of their talk: "Frosty's okay", "Don't cry", "He'll be back next year", "It's okay Alex", "He's made out of magic snow". They sure do love my little boy. Needless to say, not a sign of a tear this time, he was eating up all the attention.

He was trying hard to eat up all our rocket candies too. We had to be careful. For instance, he'd try for one candy pill if he went to the potty and nothing happened, two if something happened. Not negotiable Alex. It didn't help that one day we found ourselves giving Amy one every time we gave one to her brother. That was a mistake, a bit of mismanagement there.

Alex had his own management problems – he kept losing them. Once when he couldn't find one that I had just given him, I suggested –

"Maybe Blacks Eyes ate it."

Unhesitatingly he replied –

"No, she don't know how to open her mouth."

All right. If Blacks Eyes didn't eat it, and you didn't eat it, then where is it? Staying on top of the process was a challenge for everyone.

Was it all worthwhile, did it work? Of course it did. It worked in the same way that if you close your eyes you'll go to sleep. Maybe not as soon as you'd like, but eventually, you will go to sleep. And it worked in that it gave us a sense of doing something. That was important because his toilet training seemed to take forever.

Over the many months, we finished the rocket candies from his Halloween bag, finished all sorts of bought packs of them, and switched to gum when that became his choice. Then one day we found out that more than anything else, Alex wanted to wear underpants. Of course we were excited by this since this was our objective too. So underpants would be the next sop, and we bought him a package of three, all different colours. All he had to do was show us he was deserving, let us know he was ready. Weeks went by, not ready yet. More weeks, still not ready, and then – we had a brand new package of hand-me-downs. He'd outgrown them! Alex, please. When are you going to use the toilet?

*   *   *   *   *

I used to wonder if we bought him underpants and an electric razor at the same time, which would he find a use for first? Here we are, well into summer, working hard on a process that began half a year ago. What's happening? He grasps all that is going on so well, intellectually. He seems to. Practically, he needs a diaper change four or five times a day. Amy was quicker, the boy down the street was quicker, even I was quicker. Probably. I must have been.

It's frustrating –

Of course, it doesn't help that Amy really was so good. At this age in her young life, kerplunks and tinkle tinkle were ringing out all over the place. All we hear from Alex are comments. For instance, I was just home from work one day and I asked –

"Did you use the potty today?"

"No. I used the bathroom in my diaper."

Saturday morning, I said to him as he ran by –

"Alex, do you want to use the potty?"

"No. I don't have time to use the potty."

WHAT! What sort of an answer is that? I can't believe I heard that.

"ALEX! Come back here right...."

No use, he was gone. He was in a hurry. We'll be talking about this one – he and I – that's for sure. Here's a small exchange we had over and over –

"Alex, do you need to use the potty?"

"It's too late."

This became a stock answer for Alex. He used it all the time. Of course, each time he did, it meant that yes, it was too late, and off we'd go to the change table.

I was his teacher, so I worked with him for awhile on standing rather than sitting. I even found something for him to step up on so he'd be over the edge. I told him, "This is how men do it." I was just trying to add a little motivation.

One day, Lynn had led him to the bathroom, and he was sitting on the potty when I walked in. He said –

"This is how Kelly teach me to pee."

KELLY YOU STAY OUT OF THIS! Kelly is my five-year-old niece, what does she know.

The frustration was annoying. He seemed to understand exactly what he was putting us through – "us" being the diaper-changer, the cleaner upper. We could tell him about the embarrassment that he should feel, the cost, the irritability that he was creating, the mess – yuck! – and he would nod at all the right times. He understood everything we said! What's happening? It was sad.

Here's a little discussion on the never-ending change table, I was dressing him after a bath. He's very patient, he never tells me to hurry up. I asked him –

"Do you have to go potty?"

"No."

"Alex, are you going to start telling me if you have to go potty?"

"No."

"Alex. That's not acceptable. *When* are you going to start telling me?"

"*Soooon.*"

"When?"

"When me say so."

"When you say what?"

"When me say me have to go potty."

That's when. He's not one to be tied down. At least I had his attention. Other times he'd ignore me and change the topic first chance he had. One moonless night, he was looking out the window as he lay there. He couldn't see the big thermometer on the tree outside like he could in the daytime. I was talking, Alex interrupted –

"Alex, you really should begin to…."

"Could you turn off the dark?"

He wanted to see the thermometer. And his comments were so nonchalant. That didn't help a bit.

"If we sit down, we poop. And some day we pee standing up."

Oh my, how the learning progresses.

Grandpa once gave him a good scolding about this juvenile habit of his, pooping in his diaper. Later on the change table, long after Grandpa had gone home to Ottawa – and a few times afterwards as well – he'd remember that. He'd talk about Grandpa, and he'd say –

"Grandpa is mad."

It didn't bother him in the least. Grandpa's problem, not his.

Little ones have a direct line to their grandparents, wise people experienced as to just when it's time to move from diapers to underpants. Here is Grandma's and Grandpa's chance to get back at their children for what they did to them two or three decades earlier. Isn't it nice to be a grandparent when it comes to toilet training? A spectator role, well removed from the line of action, and called upon as a consultant from time to time: "Not yet." "Not yet." "Not quite yet."

Not long ago, Lynn and I had a glimmer of hope. Alex had become interested in toilet paper; surely he'd soon want to learn to use it. But no, not at all – it was just another toy, wouldn't you know it. He'd walk out of the bathroom with the end of a roll in his hand, and if we didn't move quickly, by the time he walked into the kitchen we'd see the other end coming out of the bathroom too. "Oh no, he's doing it again!" Exhausting, very frustrating – we were very tired.

Joy noticed this, and said –

"Don't worry. He just needs more time."

Thanks Joy. Actually, we're not worried. We're quite exasperated, a little blasphemous in a quiet way, mildly suicidal from time to time, and wishing we could move far away and go to sleep.

Daddy's wacko and sound asleep....Zzzzz.....

Dad had just changed Alex (one more time, was it the fourth or fifth time today?), sat down in a soft chair, fell asleep, and had a dream....Zzzz

"Nineteen years old, that's hard to believe. Happy Birthday Alex!"

"Thanks for the razor Dad, it works great."

"Glad you like it son. Where are you off to?"

"I'm going out with some friends."

"Are you okay for diapers?"

"Yeah, I've got a six-pack."

"Oh. I didn't know they packaged them in six-packs."

"Come on Dad, look at how big they are. If they put any more in a pack, I couldn't get through doors."

WAKE UP DAD! HE'S ONLY TWO YEARS OLD!! Two years ten months and some number of days actually, when is he going to use the toilet. Daddy's so tired with his kids, he's even wacko when he sleeps.

*   *   *   *   *

The upside and the downside of early parenting tend to come together here. It's a dangerous mix and you have to try hard to keep them separate. You always want to be sensitive to those not infrequent moments of warmth. While there are many, each is as wonderful as another, and you should try not to miss even one. Don't miss the beauty of "I love you mommy" because you're tired and on your way to the change table one more time.

It's frustrating – but is it ever cute!

Is it ever! Alex's enthusiasm knew no bounds when there were candy pills and a smile on Dad's or Mom's face to be earned. He'd be so excited. Amy told him, "Drink more water Alex, that makes you go pee." He came running to me with a cup, "Me want water!" On the double, with great excitement and anticipation, he'd head off to the bathroom. "The bathroom's in the washroom!" And when I went in to see how he was doing –

"I have to go again when I finish this. I have to pee again."

Early this summer, he'd try to go as often as we wanted to mention it. I told him he was a good boy, he peed on the potty. He replied – "I DIIIDD! Youcangivemetwocandypills." No I can't. You know what you have to do for two. And I'd hear kerplunk. And I'd hear a two-year-old's observation to boot. "That was too much." He'd hang on to his frosty and say –

"That was a whole bunch."

And then he'd pop it into his mouth.

The imagery that accompanies toilet training is unsurpassable. One day Alex – Alex the philosopher, that is – was sitting on the toilet. I was standing waiting for him and he offered the following –

"Do you know what makes me poop more? Hammer me on the
    back. I hammered Amy on the back once and she pooped
    more."

Maybe this is the embryo stage of bathroom privacy. It has nothing to do with modesty, it's simply a question of self defense.

"Diapers" to "underpants" was what it was all about, and as time went by, Alex found there were milestones to be reached along the way. He knew you couldn't put a pair of underpants over a diaper; you had to take the diaper off first. So for him, he'd reached one of these milestones when he was allowed to sport a "bare bum bum".

He'd be so excited. He'd jump out of the tub and run around grinning and screaming "I'm wearing a bare bum bum!" It didn't matter if it was past his bedtime and he should have been behaving like the utterly exhausted boy he was. He loved it. He and I had this little talk one day –

"I'm wearing a bare bum bum."

"No you're not, I just changed you."

"Yes I am."

"No."

"Yes. It's in my diaper."

He wanted so much to wear a bare bum bum that this time anyway, that was it. Here's some more of that vivid imagery. Imagine –

Alex was sitting on the potty again. He spent a lot of time doing this of course, and we'd all take turns encouraging him. He was sitting on the potty, with no clothes on, with his three cousins from downstairs huddled around encouraging him to go. But he couldn't. And then just a short while later, he was running around the living room – bare bum bum and all – with Lauren, Kristen, and Kelly all chasing the little nudie, thinking he was about to pee all over the carpet.

The bathroom with the potty was like a home within a home. I was with him on one of those occasions when he really, really wanted to go. He was trying so hard.

"Could you help me poop? Please Daddy? Could you help me?"

What could I do? I held his hands and squeezed them a little. Nothing happened, but he told me anyway, very warmly, "I want *two* candy pills, two *big* ones." I gave them to him. What's more, there was nothing quite as disarming as Alex's smile when he'd been sitting there for a long, long time. Finally it would happen – tinkle tinkle, little star – and then, truly a beautiful smile. He could clean me out of candy pills all at once when that happened.

Alex was gaining confidence every day as summer passed by. He was behaving a little less humbly, more like a boss. He was in charge. He'd say things like –

"You could wipe my bum bum ONLY. I'll flush the toilet."

So I'd wipe him up and he'd flush the toilet. It must have been around that time when I asked him if he wanted to use the potty and he told me he didn't have time. *That* took a lot of confidence. It was very funny too. What an answer! Priorities – we all have trouble with them at some time or other, don't we. I didn't know it began so early.

Gradually, "It's too late" gave way to "It's not too late now", when asked. He still had to be asked. This became his calling card when it was time to head for the potty. He'd run, and he'd shout, "It's not too late now!" He liked this assortment of words, having used the shorter version – the one without "not" – sadly, so often in the past.

We were getting closer and closer. Then one day, as cute as could be, he asked me, "When I go peep, can I have some red underwear on?" *Underpants*! Are we there? I know, "red underwear *off*" is a better idea, but then I think that's what he really meant. Maybe not. Regardless, we went right away to the underwear store and bought him two pairs of red ones.

*　　*　　*　　*　　*

However.

When you hop out of bed in the morning, just about the first thing you put on are underpants. Right? Me too. We all do. Except Alex. He's not ready, he's *still* not ready. He *wants* to put them on, and in fact, he even has some. They're in the bottom of a drawer in our room. That's where we put the red ones we bought last week in a foolish moment of great optimism. You see, we just can't wait for Alex to master toilet training. As one child became two, it's now been over four years of dealing with diapers. The arithmetic is easy: if I live to be eighty, I will have spent five percent of my life changing diapers every day!

Or pull-ups, or training pants – the process is quite sophisticated. In the beginning, it's diapers. You resign yourself and you don't even think of not changing diapers. Fair enough, you asked for it, but must it go on forever? Alex sure would like to move on to something else, and so would I.

Underpants!

Sunday mornings are lazy ones. In our bedroom upstairs we have a big window that offers a very fine view, resplendent in the early light. We have a really big bed where there's plenty of room for Amy and Alex and Lynn and Danny and Scott and me. Rub-a-dub-dub, six pigs in a tub. And we have "coffee hour", and we have a lot of fun with the kids.

"I want to wear underpants."

Guess who said that.

"I'm sorry Alex, we don't have any underpants for you."

He didn't know about the red ones hidden away. He wasn't ready yet, so we hadn't brought them out.

"Yes we do, me can wear....AMY'S underpants!"

Amy had something to say about that –

"No you can't."

"Yes, me can."

"NO YOU CAN'T! They're too big."

Lynn told Amy that her underpants probably would fit Alex, they wouldn't be too big, but Amy was adamant –

"NO!!"

Looks like we have a small problem here. It's not insurmountable, nor does it actually require resolution. It's just another step in our toilet-training effort that we would like to deal with in a forward-moving fashion. Wouldn't you?

Out of the blue, Lynn said –

"Alex, you can wear mine."

Really. And I was thinking forward-moving. So. We don't have a problem after all, he can wear his mother's. This could be interesting.

Alex was wearing only his pajama tops at this point, we were still working on how to cover his bottom. But when Lynn made her offer, he took off the tops too and was wearing nothing when she handed him her underpants. He put them on, first one foot, then the other. Then he pulled them up absolutely as high as he could, away above his waist – and commented –

"See! My peeper's in my underpants!"

No it's not! If you happened to notice, his peeper was about the only part of him from the top of his legs to his chin that *wasn't* in his underpants. We noticed, and we laughed, we laughed hard and Alex was inspired. He ran across the room in front of the bed, and in the few short steps it took, the underpants fell down to his ankles.

He stepped out and started all over. Only this time he put both feet in one leg, and when he pulled them up, the whole works went straight to his armpits. There was no ambiguity at all, and you could tell at a glance which parts were in or out – they were all out! We laughed and laughed. At one point, Amy was laughing so much, she turned to me and said as best she could, "Daddy, I couldn't stop laughing". And then she turned back and laughed some more. So there we were, all of us, laughing at Amy's little brother about as hard as we could, and you really couldn't fault us: he looked ridiculous! We just couldn't stop laughing.

And then – there was Alex. Our dear, dear Alex, our little boy. Our "little star". We love you so much. Yes, there was Alex, having the time of his young life, laughing harder than any of us. His world was turning perfectly, toilet training could wait. He knew that. Moreover, we were out of rocket candies and he knew that too. Thanks for the entertainment pal, my little funny friend.

11

Canada Day was a good holiday this summer, a happy celebration among good friends. Around supper time, many of us at the lake came together with lawn chairs, food, drink, others who were visiting, and red and white Canada flags for waving. There was a small beach and the little ones could splash about and play in the sand. We waited and waited until dark for the fireworks, so it was later than usual for them. No yawning though, none at all – just buckets of fun on a fine warm summer evening.

It was the first time Amy and Alex ever watched fireworks, and how exciting it was with all the brightness and sparkling, all the hissing and booms and screams, quiet waiting for the next one, faces suddenly looking up, BOOM again, screams again, wide eyes shining from overhead bursts, coloured balls shooting awaaaaaaaaay into the black sky!

Alex wanted to know when the red ones would be coming down. I said I'd tell him next year. When it was all over, home and once again – bedtime.

More special moments at bedtime

"Daddy."

"Yes, I'm coming. What do you want?"

"Um, I just….. um….um. Who put that coaster there?"

"I don't know."

"Did you?"

"No."

"Did I?"

"I don't know."

"Maybe I did."

"Maybe."

"Maybe Amy did."

"Maybe."

"Maybe Mommy did."

"Maybe."

"Maybe the Canada flag did."

Did he say Canada flag? I think it's time to leave.

"Yes Alex. The Canada flag put the coaster there, now go to sleep."

I walked out of his room. Family members are okay, there are only so many of us. But when he turned from people to flags, I had to leave. He was becoming more imaginative and less sleepy by the moment. If he had suggested "Maybe Scott" or "Maybe Danny", maybe I'd have stayed a little longer. Yes Alex, I saw the Canada flag put the coaster there, go to sleep.

I wonder what a Canada flag looks like when it's putting a coaster on a bedside table. The reality of inanimate objects has been with me since I was three or thereabouts, and that's a long time ago. I forget and I can't imagine. Alex can though, or so it would appear to one listening closely to his words.

He's tired. Bedtime. What a good time to check a little one's conceptual progress. Little minds are stretched trying hard to stay awake. Here's a good stretch –

"Would you lie down with me again?"

"Okay, just for a minute."

"A minute is a long time."

"No, not too long."

"Just a little bit long, but not too much."

You have to agree, his summary comment on how long is a minute was rather vague. It was a very good stretch.

I think the vagueness started with Amy when she first began to talk. She would say, "Me want apple juice" just before bed. I would reply, "Okay, just a little bit", and Amy would counter – carefully, not to contradict me – with, "Big much little bit". I'd pour some apple juice. Was it "big", was it "much", was it only "little", or was it just a "bit"? Totally vague. We heard "big much" over and over when these two were little.

In the same tradition, Alex described a minute as being "Just a little bit long, but not too much" – all these relative words reflecting a child's grappling with matters of scale. He probably thought that if he used them all at once, he would be at least partly right.

And he *really* wanted to be right. He was always trying, trying as hard as he could and telling us exactly what he thought was right. One evening just before bed, we were looking for a movie he could watch should he be first up in the morning. I found one that I remembered his enjoying back in the spring before we moved to the cottage. I said to him –

"Here's one you haven't seen for a long time."

"Yes I DID. In Ottawa."

"Yes, but not for a long time."

"It was a short time."

Wasn't that a nice try? Alex thought if he hasn't seen it for a long time, then it must have been a short time. Boy, does he have a lot to learn.

*   *   *   *   *

When Amy was two, Lynn and I would take turns lying down with her at bedtime to "talk day". That's what we called it. With that as our introduction, we'd go back and forth on all sorts of activities and talk about all the fun we'd had that day.

When we started doing this with Alex, just last May or June, "talk day" became "do the talks" and the ritual became a very important one for the young fellow. We'd begin with one of us saying something like –

"Let's start all the talks."

"You go first."

"No, you go first."

That would be our start – a little argument. It didn't matter though, because either he or I would then say, "What did we do today?" Sometimes I'd say, "What did you do today?" Regardless, we both always understood it would be Alex's doings about which we'd be talking.

Yesterday, today, and tomorrow

But that never seemed to take up enough time for him. He'd want to explore "yesterday" and "tomorrow", maybe "last night" if he could squeeze it in. He would ask questions like "What did we do yesterday?", though just as often it would be "What are we going to do yesterday?" Or, "What did we do tomorrow?"

If he happened to get "tomorrow" right, as he would sometimes, he'd say, "What are we going to do tomorrow?" And we would do a little planning. Don't think for a moment though that he had a grasp of the concept of "tomorrow". Far from it.

Alex loved to "do the talks". Not often would he get the question straight, but he sure was enthusiastic.

"Daddy, I want you to lie down again. I want you to talk again.
All of the talks. You forgot to talk all of the talks. What did
we do last night?"

So we talked about that a bit, and with the first pause, it was –

"What did we do tomorrow? Let's start the talks."

It was almost as if he had a checklist. He'd say –

"You haven't done all the talks. You did last night and tomorrow but you didn't do today and yesterday."

Another time, this is what came out –

"What are we going to do did?"

He tripped over his own exuberance. Once he said –

"What are we going to do today?"

Not much little boy Alex, lying here beside me in the dark. Sleep is about all that's left on your agenda. Here's another variation on his almost-getting-the-primary-question-right –

"What did we do today?"

Almost? That sounds exactly right, doesn't it. However. It was the first thing he said one morning, sleepily, as he struggled to open his eyes in the early light.

Once he had a trick question. I began –

"Alex, tell me what you did today."

"What did YOU do today?"

I didn't have to respond, I just had to laugh with him and enjoy his joke.

He had difficulty with the questions for a long time, but never any trouble with the answers. Of course not, he used the same answer for them all: "I went to school." He enjoyed so much his first experience with preschool in the spring. It made him feel as though he fitted right in with other little people he knew who went to school every day – his cousins, and Amy of course.

What did we do today? "I went to school." Yesterday, last night – same answer: "I went to school." What are you going to do tomorrow? "I went to school." Wrong Alex, tomorrow is Saturday, it's July, school's out. "I went to school" went on for the longest time. What a way to spend a summer holiday.

One evening, there was a variation. Amy had joined us, we were all together and she wanted to be involved. In fact, she started –

"What did we do today?"

Alex wasted no time reclaiming his turf –

"No! I want MOMMY to do it."

A compromise was needed right away –

"It's okay Alex, let Amy ask just one question."

She looked at him and said again –

"What did we do today Alex?"

"Nothing."

Yes. Different – a variation. A pleasant change from "I went to school".

Of course this was just his opener, and it would then be for Lynn or me to pry him away from it so our talks could have some substance. As summer passed by, Alex gave up thinking about answers, or even trying harder to understand the question. He'd wait for the prying, and then fall in wherever that would lead. He sure had trouble with the concept of yesterday, today, tomorrow.

On the other hand, Amy seemed quite clear on the matter. She's a year-and-a-half older than Alex so that would explain it. We didn't use this terminology when Amy was Alex's age, but we certainly did this summer with our four-year-old. The problem was that Alex would hang around – of course he would – and we'd try to explain it to him too. It was a challenge. We could have waited for him to age some, except it was very fun. Other approaches were worth a try as well.

One of Alex's solutions to his difficulty with the concept of "tomorrow" was to use the expression "after bed". This worked quite well, and we began to hear "after bed" about as frequently as we heard "I went to school".

"Let's have a bath because we're going to Stevie's party
tomorrow."

"After bed, is it tomorrow?"

"Yes."

"Then can we go to Stevie's party?"

"Yes."

"Yeaaah!"

He understood. Of course, there was a party at stake here and the need not to miss that might have added a little clarity to his perspective. Alex loves parties. So this worked well for awhile, though we had to be careful when it was time for a nap. He'd have one, and then when he awoke he'd be all ready for whatever we said we'd do "tomorrow".

Another approach was to use the days of the week. We were optimistic. The concept seemed simple – they all have names, there are only seven, and they have an order. Alex picked up a toy with which he was playing and said –

"The day AFTER tomorrow, I'll be finished playing with this."

"What day is that?"

"I don't know."

"Well, today's Sunday. What's the next day?"

"Tomorrow?"

The concept still seemed simple; we remained optimistic. Sure enough, it wasn't long before Alex showed signs of gaining confidence in his knowledge of days of the week – some of them anyway. As well, he was being exposed to more concepts all the time. Numbers and counting was a new one for him.

He listened very closely one night while I was talking with Amy about this. She knew how to go from 20 to 30, and we talked about how after 30 comes a bunch of numbers and then 4-zero, more numbers, then 5-zero, 60, 70, and so on all the way up to – a hundred! When we reached a hundred, Alex had something to say. He'd been very quiet for some time, he was listening and learning. He could contain himself no longer. Here's what he said –

"And after a hundred comes Tuesday!"

Yes. His knowledge of some of the days of the week was a fact. "Tuesday" was a good one.

Daddy's wacko yesterday, today, and tomorrow

Courteous, patient, exhibiting a sincere interest in my son's growth and learning – that's me. Right?

Wrong. It's bedtime. I'm tired – a tough day. His answer is tired – "I went to school" over and over and over. It was fun for awhile, then a little fatiguing, and finally I came to perceive this discussion the way Alex probably had seen it all along: here's how to put off going to sleep.

At bedtime last night, that being Friday, we were doing the talks. We talked about what we'd do "tomorrow", that being Saturday. We decided we'd go swimming. So at breakfast this morning, Saturday, I said –

"We're going swimming today after breakfast."

Alex looked up and said –

"We're going swimming toMORROW."

He was confused. Again. I know that's exactly what I said, Alex, but it was last night when I said it. He needed some help, I went on –

"Alex, you forgot. I said yesterday that we're going swimming
   tomorrow, but now that today is tomorrow, we're going
   swimming today. Tomorrow we're not going swimming
   because it's supposed to rain, so when tomorrow comes, and
   today is yesterday, you'll be glad we went swimming today.
   Now what would you like to do tomorrow?"

"I went to school."

I give up. Maybe Amy should teach him. I need a day off.

*   *   *   *   *

One more special moment at bedtime with Alex, master of the concept of callbacks

I would have thought there was nothing he could say that would entice me back to his room again that night. He tried hard, but his efforts were becoming increasingly subdued. I'd been back twice already – no more. I was tired, I was resisting, I was determined – in a word, I was finished. I was even beginning to be a little angry. Then he said it. He said it loudly and clearly. He mustered up all his remaining energy for this one last attempt, and I had to go back. I had no choice. Congratulations Alex, master of callbacks –

"Daddy, if you don't come and lie down with me, I'm going to go right to sleep!"

I had to go back and look at his beautiful face one more time before he closed his eyes. I smiled at him one more time, and I lay down. And one more time I heard him quietly say "Daddy I love you" but that was all. He was off to sleep in a moment.

I lay on my side with him for another four or five minutes. I listened to his soft breathing and my eyes rested on his still face. I thought about how much fun we'd all had with our soon-to-be-three-year-old's attempts to understand. I thought about how Lynn and I were so emotionally fulfilled since Amy, then Alex, had joined us. Our lives seemed complete now. I had thought my love for Alex couldn't be any greater. Now I thought about how it had just grown again with his words, with his very being. Sleep well little boy.

12

Here it is mid-July already. Next week, I'll commute to my work each day and Lynn will be with the kids, but this week it's my turn. For the third year in a row, the kids and I are going to drive to Ottawa Monday morning, and on to Tweed. We have a couple of other stops to make along the way, and then back home on Friday. But wouldn't you know it – bad timing this year.

It has to do with Amy's reluctance to sleep in her own bedroom. Since we moved to our cottage almost a month ago, she really hasn't accepted that it is indeed her room. Perhaps this is because it has a double bed and becomes our guest room whenever we have company. On these occasions, she comes upstairs and sleeps with us. She'd like to come upstairs every night, but that's not allowed. Sometimes, she'll start upstairs and I'll carry her down when she's asleep, other times we insist she sleeps in her own room from the beginning. She resists.

On the other hand, Alex's room is great – bunk beds, he loves it. His is the lower bunk. Well, a couple of nights ago, we looked at the possibility of Amy sleeping in the upper. She could stay there until she feels that she is ready to move back into her own room. Alex doesn't mind, and we persuaded Amy that as a roommate, he's okay. That wasn't hard to do because Alex always has been special to Amy. So it seems our small dilemma has been settled at last and Amy is comfortable with the result. Last night she was, anyway. But now we're off on our trip; we'll just have to wait and see.

First we had to pack, and we began as soon as Lynn left for work this morning. Alex packed Blacks Eyes, I looked after the rest, and Amy took a couple of bags out and was first one into the car when we were set to go an hour or two later. Say goodbye to the dogs Alex. Mom will be home tonight to feed them.

"Goodbye Scott, goodbye Danny. We're going on a trip."

"And where are we going on our trip, Alex?"

"Which one?"

I'm glad he's not driving. Come on, climb in, we're going now.

*　　*　　*　　*　　*

Pokin' on the road

It's a pretty drive heading south to Ottawa. First there are a few miles of winding, hilly, country roads, and then you breeze into Ottawa on a highway and a big bridge over the Ottawa River. Turn right and on to Tweed, we should be there for dinner. Normally, it's a three-hour drive from Ottawa to Tweed, but when you poke, it's more like five. And when you have a couple of dawdlers – two- and four-year-olds, for example – you poke.

Lynn's mom and dad go to Tweed every summer for a few weeks. They stay in a quiet, big old house right beside Lake Stoco. There's room for everyone, always enough beds, and we're all so very welcome. We're going to visit for three nights, and it sure is going to be fun! Maybe Lynn's sisters, Jane or Laurie or both, will show up with some cousins to play with Amy and Alex. You never know.

It wasn't long before Ottawa was behind us and we were pokin' along a little faster. Soon it was lunchtime and we all were hungry. I could never figure out these along-the-way meals. I'd always buy what everyone seemed to want, but this would be too much and we'd have leftovers. Such a waste. I talked with Joy about this before we left, and she suggested I just buy something for the kids and then finish up whatever they leave. That sounded like a good idea.

So I bought a hot dog and fries for each of them and for drinks, Amy chose milk and Alex orange juice. We drove to a roadside stop and sat down at a picnic table. Guess who ate all their lunch? Amy and Alex did, that's who. That's okay, I knew we'd be pokin' along to an ice cream store awhile later – I love ice cream – and Amy and Alex always have extra for their dad.

Whenever Alex drinks orange juice, I'm reminded of what happened one weekend last February. It was very dramatic, and a few weeks later, very funny too. Amy had a sleepover at Rachel's house, Lynn had some things to do in town, and we thought it might be fun for Alex and I to carry on with some serious bonding. So the two of us, and Scott and Danny, headed off to the cottage Friday night. Alex was quite thirsty Saturday morning and he began with two cups of orange juice. Just a little while later we were playing on the big bed upstairs when suddenly, up came the orange juice, all of it, all over me and the bed. Well, that was the start of it. Alex was ill all weekend, and the predominant male-bonding activity turned out to be doing laundry.

Three or four weeks later, with his still uncluttered memory, Alex recalled all of this – at the dinner table yet. We were talking about going to the cottage again, and he began to talk in his quick, abrupt and continuous manner, and it went something like this: "Daddy and me went to the cottage and me sick all over the bed but me not sick anymore, see?" With that, he looked right at each of us in turn with his mouth open about as wide as it could be. Nothing came out. He's not sick anymore, he's absolutely right. Phew. That's about as serious a proclamation of good health as you'll ever find offered up by a two-year-old: a few words followed by a live, visual demonstration. Well done young fellow.

Yes, his hot dog and fries were all gone. Alex told us how he ate his fries –

"I ate one at a time, and then another one at a time."

As for his orange juice –

"I didn't like my orange juice so I drank it all."

Not even a drop for Dad. Amy too, finished everything. Then she said –

"Look, I didn't spill."

"Good, I'm glad you didn't spill."

Alex – Alex the philosopher, that is – added –

"You're glad she don't, but if she do, then you're not glad she
    don't."

We cleaned up and climbed back into the car and back on the highway. It
was a gorgeous summer day, pokin' was just fine. It wasn't long before we
came to a small beach by Silver Lake and we all agreed that stopping for a
swim was the thing to do.

Whenever I swim, I'm one who likes to get wet all at once. So as soon as
we were in our bathing suits, I said –

"I'm going to run and run and run and run and dive."

Amy's turn –

"I'm going to run and run and run and not dive. I'm going to do
    that."

And she did.

Alex sauntered in. He'd found an old set of plastic measuring spoons
someone had left in the sand and walked in, playing with them. He filled
one with water and lifted it towards his mouth....

"ALEX DON'T DRINK THAT WATER!"

"'Cause then it will be all gone and there'll be no more water in
    the pool and we won't be able to swim here anymore."

That's right. And when we're thirsty again, we'll just have to find another
pool. Dad and his little kids sure had fun at the swimming stop that day.

Conversations with a four-year-old

Off we went again, next stop – ice cream. It was very
quiet now, we were all a little tired. We couldn't go
faster than pokin' even if we wanted to. Alex fell asleep
and Amy explained to me why that happened –

"Do you know what? It's a long road. That's
    why he's sleeping."

So Amy and I settled in for a little talk. She was beside me in the front. I talked about the time Alex had been ill, orange juice all over the bed. Amy, do you remember what he told us when he was better? No, she didn't remember, and I told her about that too. She laughed.

"Do you know what? I feel like I'm sick but I'm not sick. Do you know why I'm not sick? Because I have the hiccups."

Did she ever. But only for a little while and then it was quiet again.

"Daddy don't nap."

"Are you going to nap?"

"No, I'm not that tired. Do you know why?"

"Why?"

"Because when we get to the ice cream store, I'm not going to nap."

Amy loves ice cream almost as much as I do.

Soon, Alex woke up and we stopped at a little store with a big ice cream cone on its sign. We each ordered one.

"The vanilla is in the chocolate!"

– exclaimed Alex as he had a bite of his ice cream that had been dipped in chocolate. It was a hot day and Alex's vanilla traveled. It began in the chocolate, and from there, it headed on into his tummy, onto his shirt, down his arm, and the last bite or two – pop, right into my mouth. Ymm.

We sure were enjoying the pace, and we poked some more as we headed off down the road. Alex was wide awake now. I had a couple of shiny nickels, and I passed them back so he could play with them. He wondered –

"Did you buy them at work?"

Now how do you answer a question like that? You don't, you just smile. That's what I did. A few miles further we slowed down going through a town, and I talked to them about stop signs and traffic lights. He wondered about these too –

"Where are the 'Go' signs?

He must be a little kid, look at all those questions. Amy had brought along her tape player, so we listened to some music. Between songs, she said to Alex, sitting directly behind her in the back seat –

"Alex, if you want to listen to a different tape, I could put on one."

"I want to listen to a different tape."

"This one?"

"Yeah, that one."

He must be a very little kid. He had no idea which tape she had in her hand because he couldn't see it.

The sun was pokin' too, still high in the sky when we pulled into Grandma's driveway. We were about a half hour later than we said we'd be arriving for dinner, but that's okay. Grandparents know what poking is all about. Soon everything was unpacked and in the house and after dinner, it was almost bedtime. They both turned in quickly – a couple of sleepy kids. Alex said –

"Do you know why I'm tired? Because I had a busy day."

"Did you have a fun day?"

"No I had a BUSY day."

"But did you have fun too?"

"Yes I had a fun day but I didn't have a busy day."

Oh Alex, I'm sorry. You can have fun and be busy at the same time! You didn't know that, did you. We're going to be really busy tomorrow, so you have a good sleep. And you just watch how much fun we have tomorrow too!

*　　*　　*　　*　　*

At Grandma's house by Lake Stoco

It takes all of two minutes to walk from Grandma's house to a small, beautiful park. The kids love it. There's a play structure, lots of grass, swings and teeter-totters, and a small beach – you can play and play and then cool down in the lake, and then play again on the beach. And by the beach, there's some shade and picnic tables for the older set, people like me. So that's where we went right after breakfast Tuesday.

Later in the morning Laurie came for a visit, and when she showed up at the park, Alex had a question for her. I'm sure it was something she'd never been asked before. It was another super day, and she'd put on a bikini for some sun and a swim. Alex hadn't seen too many bikinis, or if he had, he hadn't noticed their construction. Or if he had noticed this – he hadn't commented. But he did this time. What do you suppose he said? What does a young man say to a lady wearing a bikini? A very young man, that is. Give up?

"Aunt Laurie, why are you wearing two bathing suits?"

Just a little comment on Alex's prowess at counting. It has nothing to do with his prowess at assessing the fashion tastes of a young lady wearing her bathing suit(s). That can wait. There goes Alex up the beach. He's probably scouting around for someone wearing three or four bathing suits. Alex seems a bit slow coming to understand the concept of a bathing suit. Maybe by summer's end, we'll see.

Here's a concept that he did grasp early on: if you get something, you can lose it. He would lose things from time to time, so we'd talk about this. Once he got a haircut.

"I hear you got a haircut from Grandma."

"Yes. And I still have it."

Now it's almost four weeks later and we're with Grandma once again. Amy was talking about getting a haircut, and naturally enough, Alex wanted one too. He always wants what Amy has or is about to have. But he remembered this one he'd received not long before, so there was only one way in his mind he might possibly be able to get another. He came to me and said –

"Daddy, I lost my haircut."

"You did?"

"Yes, it's gone."

"Where?"

"I don't know."

"Did you lose it indoors or outdoors?"

"I don't know."

He had a very perplexed look on his face, and I questioned him no further. I explained that you don't "lose a haircut", and yes, he needed another one, and yes, he could have one along with Amy. And Tuesday evening, when Aunt Laurie headed back to Ottawa after dinner, Grandma cut two small blond heads of hair. Amy reminded me of that a week or two later when I heard her say –

"Mommy, do you remember when Alex used to say to Grandma 'My haircut's all gone, could you give me another one?' because he *loves* haircuts."

*   *   *   *   *

On our trip, Alex peed in a variety of places: toilets, bushes, probably in lakes even though I told him not to, twice in an "out-of-house" as he calls it, and elsewhere no doubt. And he peed at the park. This was the most interesting of all because it had a social dimension. It came as no surprise though. You see, he's toilet trained! He's proud and he loves to talk about it.

While there have been relapses, and I'm sure there will be more, I like to think that Alex's toilet training ended on Sunday about a week before we left on our trip. I had a hint a few days earlier that this was soon to happen. Lynn came home from shopping and said, "I just spent a fortune on diapers." Same idea as how it never rains when you take along an umbrella. So I was really pleased when she said this, and started thinking right away whom we knew who could use all the extra diapers we were about to have.

We had company at the cottage that weekend and there was much commotion. Amidst it all, Lynn went upstairs and the bathroom door was closed. This was very unusual. She carefully knocked and opened it, and on the other side Alex was sitting on the toilet.

"Alex, what are you doing? Did you tell anyone, did you ask
anyone to help you?"

"I just told myself. I asked myself that I had to go poop and pee.
No actually, I asked the raccoons out there that I had to go pee."

All by himself. I'm sure glad it was all okay with the "raccoons out there" (a pair of toy stuffed kangaroos sitting on Lynn's dresser). He talks like the very little boy he is, but now he poops and pees like a big one. All by himself! The long, long saga that began with the rocket candies is over. We dug out the red underpants for him that day.

A couple of days later, he announced –

"I need to go poop."

We went right away to the toilet and when he sat down, I said –

"Am I going to hear a 'kerplunk'?"

"Amy calls it 'punk', and Mommy and me call it 'plunk'."

He's quite discerning, isn't he, his knowledge is very impressive. At such a young age too! Another time, I asked him –

"Do you want to go pee on the potty?"

"You're supposed to say 'Do you need to go pee', not 'Do you
want to'."

"Do you need to go pee on the potty?"

"No."

A solid grasp of the theory, wouldn't you say? He knows it all cold. Wow. He's so good – so mature and so understanding. I'm so proud.

He's heard it so many times before, *sooo* many times.

Remember all those audible moments, all those beautiful sounds a little one makes? Here's another, it's the best. It takes awhile before the youngster learns to articulate it, but when it comes, no sound is sweeter. Our list is a little longer now: giggling, cackling, chortling, incidental humming, I need to go poop,….

At the park

Wednesday, we went back to the park. It was another beautiful day so there we were right after breakfast again. And yes, when Alex peed at the park, there was indeed a social dimension to it.

Not far from the play structure, over near the swings, is a brick building that has a drinking fountain and two good-sized washrooms. When Alex told me he had to go, that's where we went. Toilet training hasn't changed his lack of inhibition – discretion continues not to be a value for him. As we approached the facility, he commented to a middle-aged woman –

"I need to go peep."

She replied that she had the same need. A couple of minutes later as we were about to leave, he commented again, this time to a man wearing a Detroit Tigers baseball cap who had just come in –

"I went peep in THAT potty."

He pointed to the urinal he had used when I lifted him up. Once outside the door, when a couple of girls, about nine or ten I'd say, were walking by, he just had to go up to them and say –

"I went peep where Daddy does."

The two girls looked befuddled and didn't know quite what to make of this saucy young fellow's impertinence.

A short while later, I noticed a family walking together. There was a middle-aged woman, a man with a Tiger ball cap, and their two daughters

– about nine or ten I'd say. I'll bet they were talking about my son. Maybe me too. I suppose if you're going to talk to strangers about such a delicate subject, it makes sense to keep it all in a family. Did I say "delicate"? Wrong. That's what it used to be, but not anymore.

Alex is proud of his newfound capability. He said to me –

"I want to be a big boy. AND I want to be a daddy. Then I can
    pee standing up ALL THE TIME. Just like you."

What a kid, I love him.

*　　*　　*　　*　　*

Thursday's next. Everything back into the car, Amy and Alex too, me too – goodbye Grandma and Grandpa, thanks for the wonderful time! It's only an hour to Peggy's and Jim's, and later this afternoon we'll head on over to Uncle Dave's for the night. It's just another hour further.

I thought our morning drive would be non-stop, but that wasn't to be. Alex had an accident and needed some fresh underwear. He forgot to ask me to stop the car, and then it was too late. I told him –

"I'm sorry Alex. Some day soon you'll learn."

"Yeah, I will. Is that okay?"

We both felt very badly about this. I felt so sorry for him.

Engleburn Point juts a short way into the northeast corner of Stony Lake and that's where our friends have built their home. They have a boat and the swimming is terrific. There's no beach, I can dive right in! And with their water wings, the kids feel right at home. We arrived and reminisced. We talked about our trip and all the goings-on along the way, and how the kids have changed since a year ago. Live demonstrations of that were right in front of us.

The first time we drove over for a visit, Amy being two and Alex not quite a year, Jim had said, "You're brave." It was just an up-and-back day trip from Grandma's house, so Jim didn't see just how loaded was the car. And of course, he didn't see me unpack in Tweed – more than a dozen trips as I recall. I'd brought everything, as this was my way of dealing with my thinking that I wasn't brave at all. I remember Grandma and Grandpa standing on the porch with the little ones, grinning the whole time I was unpacking. That's a long time to keep a grin on your face.

Bumpy boat rides

Their boat has a flat bottom and a motor that gets it going plenty fast enough so that you feel all the bumps. "Bumpy boat ride" is what their grandchildren call it. Adults usually take along a cushion on which to sit; what a good idea that is. Each year after lunch, off we'd go for a ride.

It had been mostly a non-event for Alex his first two summers. Both times he fell asleep almost as soon as we left the dock. Of course, he wasn't even one the first time, and not quite two last year. Now he'll soon be three, and I wondered if he'd be sleeping again. Likely not. I'd even talked to him about his two previous aqua-naps. We climbed into the boat and pushed off.

Jim was in the back driving carefully, he didn't want to miss any bumps. Amy was in the middle and beside her sat Peggy with Alex on her lap. What excitement! He was having so much fun! Me too, up in the front loving every minute – the sun and wind melding with the water and trees along the shore, it was exhilarating! Then I heard "Tony", and I turned around.

Well. Another non-event for Alex – sound asleep. At least this time his nodding off came quietly. Last year he was hollering when he fell asleep. "Faster, faster! Fas…." Zonk. He was gone. Maybe next year, he'll be almost four then. Amy, come up front and sit with me. Your little brother won't be much fun for awhile.

Soon after our boat ride, we were back in the car and on our way. Alex didn't wake up. I carried him from the dock and carefully put him in his car seat. Off we went and he slept all the way to Uncle Dave's. It was day four of our trip and he was tired. When we arrived, I wakened him and asked him if he remembered falling asleep. He thought about it, and said –

"My eyes were still open and then, and then, and then….they were closed."

At Uncle Dave's

We hadn't seen Uncle Dave since New Year's Day. He'd visited us in late December for two or three days – lots of play and holiday gifts for the little ones. They love their Uncle Dave for many good reasons. I'd told the kids to wish him a Happy New Year again when he left, but Alex was a little mixed up. He said –

"Have a good year."

So far, it has been quite good, happy too, and once again the kids had a fine time with their Uncle Dave.

Conversations with a four-year-old

There were some photographs on a table in his living room, and I recognized one that I hadn't seen for a very long time. Dave must have uncovered it since the last time I visited. It was a black and white picture of he and I standing beside each other on a summer day when we were about seven or eight. The kids had never before seen a picture of their dad as a boy, so this would be fun. I showed it to Amy first –

"Amy, do you know who that is?"

"No."

"Guess. That's Uncle Dave. Who's beside him?"

"I don't know."

"Who do you think?"

"His brother?"

"Yes, and who is his brother?"

"I don't know."

"Me!"

"What was your name?"

"Tony!!"

Yes Amy, my name back then was Tony just as it is now. Can you imagine that?

Amy had some difficulty here. I wonder what she was thinking. Maybe, "No way, I know Dad and that's not him." Or maybe, "Dad's so old, he never could have been that young!" Oh well, I'll show her some more pictures another time if she doesn't believe me.

Alex, on the other hand – our little would-be-independent, full-of-himself, cute though, two-year-old – had this to say –

"Alex, do you know who this is?"

"Is that me?"

"No."

"Yes it is. Why isn't it me?"

Yes indeed, full of himself. What a rascal.

When the kids went to bed, I looked at the picture again. I like it. I think I remember the clothes I was wearing. I tried hard to remember life back then, but that's hard to do. Neither Amy nor Alex saw me in that picture at all. They saw only a couple of kids side by side who simply aren't part of their lives. I put it back on the table and turned in, thinking about bumpy boat rides and our trip home the next day.

*   *   *   *   *

Friday morning we said goodbye to Uncle Dave and drove all the way home in the rain. No poking this time, we made it in four hours. The three of us were so happy to see Mom again, and she told us she'd been counting the days. The dogs were very excited. Scott was gaga for a long, long time, Danny kept rolling over for more tummy scratches.

Home again

When it was time for bed, we all lay down in Alex's room. Mom climbed up into the top bunk with Amy, Alex and I were underneath. She remembered that the bunk beds came from her family's cottage at Constance Bay, and when she was a little girl – four years old, just like Amy – and for many years afterwards, she spent her summer nights in that same top bunk. Mom felt nostalgic –

"Lying here in my old bed with my old bedspread really makes me feel…."

"Not anymooorre!"

– said Amy.

"….makes me feel cozy and comfy."

"Not anymoorrre!!!"

– said Amy again.

"….makes me feel like a little girl again."

"NOT ANYMOOORRRE!"

– said Amy and Dad together. Mom forgot I was on the lower bunk with Alex. Amy is a bit of a wet blanket regarding this nostalgia stuff, isn't she. At Uncle Dave's, she didn't see that youthful picture ever being me. And now, we both just said "No" to Mom's backward glance. Sorry Mom. Our lives are with our children now, and they just weren't around back then.

Lynn said to Amy –

"How does it feel to be back in your own bed?"

"This isn't my bed. My bed's the big one in the other room."

Good for you Amy. She grew up a little on our trip, that's good. I asked –

"What did we do today, Alex?"

"I went to school."

– he replied, tired and smilingly. Oh yes, I forgot. I went to school. He didn't grow up, he stayed the same. That's good too. Tired and smilingly, Lynn and I went upstairs to bed ourselves. Goodnight you two.

13

As a parent, I love the dependency my children have on me. I'm an important man. And because they know they're dependent on me, they usually do as they're told, they love me, they smile when I smile, they reach for my hand when we're walking without being asked, and on and on. It's very flattering. Of course, she and he have no choice, so I don't really *feel* flattered. I feel the fun, the warmth, and the love. That's what I feel.

However, sometimes I'm not so sure about all this. Now and again, they both want to be independent so badly that I don't know how they feel about me. I can remember as a boy leaning in this direction, but wasn't that when I was a teenager? I don't remember being concerned about this in younger years. Watching the two of them every day though, it begins early. It's very cute and clearly, it's as much wanting to impress as it is to be independent.

Early pursuits of independence

We have a chair for Alex that we can attach to a table, and then put him in with confidence. We don't have to worry about the chair slipping, him falling, or other calamities. Not quite true. This is the chair from which he dropped my butter dish and that almost landed him in BIG trouble. A year or so later, he still fits the seat, but has his own ideas about the ins and outs –

"Don't help me out. You'll just have to put me back in so I can get out all by myself."

While I'm helping him back in, I'll think about how independent he's becoming. Nice try Alex, that's all it was though. You can climb out of your chair but you're still mine a few more years.

At least that many no doubt. Meanwhile, they both like to do things "ALL BY MYSELF" just as often as they can. As well, they both like to "help", in an eclectic sort of way. Now there's a recipe for trouble. I was expecting the worst one night when Amy went into the bathroom. Alex followed, that's why. But then the two of them came running out together, Amy shouting –

"I went to the bathroom ALL BY MYSELF!"

"And I helped!"

One wonders what went on in the bathroom. Not much, the toilet paper is less accessible than usual and Alex had handed her some. That's all.

One evening, Amy said enthusiastically –

"Daddy, I can do something that's really FAN-TAS-TIC!"

"What's that?"

She came over to where I was sitting, and nose-to-nose with eyes open as wide as could be, she said –

"I know how to not use a stool to wash my hands."

And then the next day –

"Do you want to not see me use the stool to wash my hands?"

"Okay."

"You'll have to turn on the light."

She knows her limitations too. She still needs a stool for turning on the light. You're going to have to be patient, you two. One little step at a time.

Patience is more difficult

In children's eyes, parents are role models, and the role we model for them is one of maturity. "This is what the finished product looks like" we tell them every day. We tell them many things explicitly. Generally, I suppose that's called "teaching". There are many other things, though, that we don't discuss nearly as often as we demonstrate. They notice and imitate – a couple of would-be grown-ups. It's such fun to watch.

"Independence" is an easy one, they do what they can. "Patience" is more elusive and Amy and Alex often don't even seem to try. Alex wasn't very patient when it came to my meting out gum on our trip. It was a daily exercise of saying "Yes" to him once, and "No" – with reasons – several times. I had to be very patient myself.

"Daddy, can we have more gum?"

It was always "we" even though Amy never asked. I think he was wanting to deflect part of my likely negative reply.

"No. I told you. I'll give you another piece tomorrow. After breakfast."

"Can I have breakfast now?"

He still doesn't understand "tomorrow". Or is it "breakfast" that he doesn't understand? One time, his mother told him he could have some gum after breakfast and at least he waited until the morning. That was it though. First thing, he came into our room and said –

"I want to wake up now Mommy. Can we have breakfast?"

Alex understands breakfast. It's what you eat in the morning before you get something good to put in your mouth.

And when Stevie had her party, we told him we'd be going there after his nap the next day. He was excited about that and the next morning, first thing again, into our room he came as soon as he was out of bed –

"Can I have my nap now?"

Patience, Alex, patience.

I had two pieces of gum left. The kids knew that, but it was almost time for bed. Here's a little talk between the two of them. For awhile, I didn't say anything – no need, the gum was in my pocket. Alex turned to me and began –

"You said we could have some gum."

Amy didn't want to be left out this time. Right away she said –

"Me too."

"First me."

Sometimes Amy thinks she's the boss. She told Alex –

"Okay, you can have some first, but I think that's enough for
today."

"No it's not."

"Yes."

"First me."

That was the second time he said "First me." Then Amy said –

"It doesn't really matter who goes first."

"First me."

"First neither of them" was what I had in mind. So I stepped in –

"Not tonight."

Amy replied –

"No, I DON'T MEAN tonight. TOMORROW."

Alex replied too –

"If the dogs might eat it, we can buy some more."

He'd like that. There would be more than two pieces then, so that would be
just fine. But what a lack of patience – "First me" three times!

Gum has been a big thing for him this summer. He had his very own
package when he began using the potty without being asked, and we told
him there'll be a package for his birthday too. Running his words
together very quickly, he said –

"Megoingtobe-BIG-andmehavemybirthdayandmehavegum."

Where there are some of those confusing concepts at play, lacking patience is so easy to see. Is "manners" one of these concepts? Grandpa was over, and he always brings a bag of peppermints with him. The kids are not allowed to help themselves, but Grandpa is very generous – to a point. Here's what he said to Alex –

"You can have one more peppermint, but no more until we go home."

"When are you going home Grandpa?"

You're being rude Alex. It's going to take a few years for Alex to learn patience. His enthusiasm for life and learning, new things and fun things – gum and peppermints – all stand in the way. As well, my demonstrations of patience often are quite subtle, hardly even noticeable. He may have missed some. I'm sure he's going to come up short on patience for some time yet. That's all right though because you don't really need it until you're trying to toilet-train your kid.

And I had just enough, what a process. Yes, I promised Alex his own pack of gum once he mastered it. So when he did, I bought him one, gave it to him, and was with him when he opened it with his friends. He was proud. He gave a piece to Kaitlyn, a piece to himself, a piece to Kaitlyn, a piece to Amy, a piece to Kaitlyn, a piece to Lindsay, and *another* piece to Kaitlyn – I think he's in love. Then Kaitlyn gave a piece to Amy. She chewed it awhile and stuck it in Amy's hair.

Our little boy sure likes Kaitlyn. It doesn't seem right to speak of a "first girl friend" when the girl just turned two, and the boy is nothing more than an almost-three-year-old, unseasoned kid. It's tempting though. We have a picture of Alex with his arm around Kaitlyn that's so warm it would melt your socks off and your hat too.

Sharing is Amy's thing

How was that for sharing by Alex? I would have thought rather good were it not for this little talk he and I had a few days later –

"Some day will you buy me a pack of gum?"

"I bought you a pack when you learned to use the potty."

"I shared it with Amy and Lindsay and Katie, but Katie wanted too much."

"And you gave her too much, didn't you."

"Yeah. So you'll have to buy me another pack."

Forget it Alex. No, in our young twosome, Amy is the one who shares. Maybe it takes four years from scratch to get the hang of it, Alex still has a year or so to go.

Conversations with a four-year-old

Preschool is a font of art and craft activities, and unless you're a little kid, it's excessive. Too much. Home they'd all come, and then they'd find their way on to Dad's or Mom's dresser, or the table in the hall, or the bulletin board in the other hall. Or face down on top of the fridge for a few days. You know. For the most part it's discretionary, Mom and Dad being the decision makers regarding placement. The "sharing" was wonderful – what an opportunity!

"Daddy. Look at these pictures. This one is for
Mommy, and this one is for you."

How many times have I been greeted thusly after a day's work. No hello, no enthusiasm, and then back to play. Sometimes it's really nice. Musically, with a fun smile, first Mom and then me –

"A – loving – present – just – for – you
A – loving – present – just – for – you."

Thanks Amy!

"Here's a picture to share. It's for you and
Mom. You have to share it."

Serves us right, doesn't it. Once when we were discussing what to take and what not to take to the cottage, Amy had this to say about her new little doll friend Molly –

"No. Molly's not coming. Do you know what?
She's bad. She doesn't share."

Sounds like Dad or Mom talking here. Amy often sounds that way.

Little kids are never stuck for an answer

Well, hardly ever. Mom and Dad are quick and so are they. Ask a question, turn your voice up a little at the end of your sentence so the kid knows for sure it's a question, and you'll get a response. You'll hear some words. Amy said to me –

"I can't wear my pink jacket."

"Why not?"

"Because the sleeves are all wet on the inside."

"Why are they wet?"

"Because I don't know."

Wasn't that a good answer? She didn't say "Because" by itself since she knew that we would then say "BECAUSE WHAT!" Ever say that? So she gave it to us all at once, and to her way of thinking, her answer was a good one – she wasn't stuck at all.

Alex never leaves a question unanswered and he's apt to be quite original. We were playing together once and he said –

"I'm your daddy."

Just a minute.

I needed to talk to him about this. I needed some clarification. I think he knew I could see through what he had just said, there was a loophole. I asked –

"You're my daddy?"

"No. I'm Amy's mom."

He changed his tune – didn't miss a beat though. And he knows how to answer a question with another question. What a good trick that is. Remember what he said when I asked him where we were going on our trip? He said, "Which one?" Excellent response, he was off the hook immediately.

I thought I was about to catch him one time when we were outdoors in our backyard in Ottawa. He was teasing Danny. She has a rubber carrot that she chases and brings back unfailingly, but Alex was sitting on it, and had been for some time. Poor Danny. So Lynn suggested that he should do things to make her happy, and with that, he took the carrot and pitched it into Jane's backyard, right over the fence. There's a gate, but it was closed.

"How's that going to make her happy?"

Now there's a difficult question. If he's ever going to be stuck, now's the time, don't you think?

"Well it will if I go and get it for her."

It's true. They're never stuck for an answer. Of course, sometimes you do have to be lenient in your acceptance of these answers. A little follow-up might be required too, such as –

"ALEX. GET THAT CARROT NOW!"

Independence, patience, sharing, not being stuck for an answer – Mom and Dad respect these values and demonstrate them regularly. Amy and Alex take it all in. Then it's their turn, and they eagerly show us what they've learned. Regularly? They try, it's fun – a little-kid approach to maturity. It's fun even when the learning is slow: not an inkling of "patience" yet.

*   *   *   *   *

Of course, there is any number of values. It's a smorgasbord. Being cool certainly is one. It's not cool to be precise or exact, so let go – "close enough" ought to do most of the time. Definitely, very cool.

Close enough, that's cool

Erin, Jeffrey, and Kevin were coming on Saturday, three more cute little kids. So we told our two about these three and this time, about Mom and Dad too. Sandy and Chuck. Saturday morning arrived and the kids were excited. I said to Alex –

"After breakfast, do you know who's coming?"

"Erin, Jeffrey, and Erin."

"No, no, you haven't got that quite right. Try again. Who's coming?"

"Everybody!"

Now you've got it! Close enough, anyway. Cool. Everybody came. A while later, I brought out some chips and said to Amy –

"Would you like some dip?"

"No."

"No what?"

"No please."

No Amy. That's not quite right. But that's okay because "please" is a polite word and we all knew exactly what she meant. So that was close enough too. And we all laughed.

When our friends went home after supper, there was still enough warm evening light in the sky for canoeing. Our lake was peaceful, very calm, and Amy and I headed down. I put the canoe in the water, and Amy said –

"Can I get in now?"

"No. The person in the stern always gets in first."

"Can I stir too?"

Close enough. That was funny. "Stern" wasn't a good choice of words, was it. However, I knew what she meant – she just wanted to do what her dad was doing.

Our canoe ride was a short one, and there was time for a quick swim. Then we went up to the cottage, and Amy told her mom and Alex exactly what we had done –

> "There were so many loons, we couldn't go swimming. Do you know what we did? We pushed some of the loons into the water, and they went down to see the fishes, and then we put the canoe in, and then went swimming."

What do you think? Her hair was wet, so we must have had a swim. I was carrying two life jackets – a strong suggestion there had been a canoe ride. And loons are no strangers to our lake, though not as abundant as Amy had said. Close enough? I don't think so. I don't think she even tried this time. How about "close enough to being a four-year-old", and that's *really* cool.

The next morning, Alex woke up and came out of his room much as he always does. Sometimes, it seems that he comes out of his room slightly ahead of when he awakens. This might have been one of those times. He went straight to Mom –

> "Amy's little sister just woke up."

> "You mean Amy's little brother."

> "Yeah, heh, heh. Daddy, I said 'Amy's little sister', and I was TRYING to say 'Amy's little sister', and …."

That was a nice try. Two nice tries, actually. And plenty close enough, don't try again Alex. We do have our slow mornings, don't we.

Alex knows lots of words, more every day, but he sometimes uses them at the wrong time. He just used "sister" when he should have used "brother". He used "idea" one time and I had no idea what he was talking about. It was last spring and I wanted to go to the cottage to do some painting. As I was about to leave, Alex said –

> "Goodbye Dad, have a good idea."

I was stumped. I was thinking about painting, not ideas. I said to him –

> "Do you have one?"

Alex was stumped. So we both were stumped. Not Mom though, she'd been listening while we were confusing each other. She cleared things up –

"I think he meant have a good *time*."

I asked him if that was what he meant and he said yes.

Not close enough. So was he cool or was he a dodo bird? Mom understood, knew exactly what he was talking about. He was cool, very mature – very close enough. I wonder what that makes me.

Friendship

"Respecting friendship" is another smorgasbord value, it's there for the picking. One lazy summer afternoon, Amy picked it and took it up the hill to Lindsay's.

It was a Friday, the last day of our holidays. We weren't ready to move home yet though because we all were having just too much plain ordinary fun. We decided to stay another week. Lynn and I would drive to Ottawa each day, and the kids would play with Kaitlyn and Lindsay. They'd spend their days at Joy's house, and at "Joy's Park" too – a sand box, a couple of swings and a slide.

So after lunch that lazy day, Alex lay down for his nap. I suggested to Amy that we might play a game of snakes and ladders, or if she'd rather, we could build her waffle house. We had talked about doing that for a couple of days now. Amy said –

"Can I go up to Lindsay's?"

I asked her to come and sit with me because I wanted to talk with her. She did. I explained about next week and how she'd be at Joy's all the time. She already knew. She listened attentively while I told her all my good reasons why her waffle house or snakes and ladders would be fun. Amy always likes a game of snakes and ladders with her dad. Then she looked right into my eyes and said –

"Please can I go up to Lindsay's?"

Of course you can, and up she went. About ten minutes later, I followed to see if this was okay with Joy, even though it always is. She told me what Amy had said when she arrived –

"Daddy told me to come up here and not come back before dinner."

Joy asked her if he really said that.

"No. That's just what I wished he'd say."

I couldn't think what to say when Joy told me that. Even had I been there at the time, I doubt I'd have thought of anything. But then, no response is needed to so many things little kids say and do. Just notice them. Enjoy them and have fun, passivity is good. Be careful with expectations – they don't have any, why should you.

14

Early friendships are special – an initial branching out socially. Of course, it's still not much more than playing with a playmate, but then, maybe that's what friendship always is, never anything more. Amy would agree. I enjoy her friendships these days. She didn't used to have any. And do you know what? Whenever she has a friend over, there's *another* cute little kid in the house.

Amy's friendship with Lindsay took off this summer. They're both four now, another year has gone by and I suppose that's why. Two little girls, only slightly apart in age, have oodles of fun things they can do together.

On the other hand, her friendship with Alex has been, well, different. There are fun things for them too, but they see each other every day and they always have. With that sort of exposure, it's hard to be always nice. Most of the time though, they get along just fine.

Conversations with a four-year-old

One evening, around the time we were getting ready to move home to Ottawa, I lay down with Amy at bedtime and asked her a question about her little brother.

"Amy, do you think Alex is cute?"

"Yes."

"Why?"

"I don't know."

"No, tell me. Why?"

"I don't know."

The next morning at breakfast, the two of them were horsing around and I asked her again –

"Do you still think Alex is cute?"

"Yes."

"Why?"

"Because he's funny."

Little kids are cute because they're funny. They sure are.

After dinner that evening, she was sitting on my lap while I tied her shoes –

"Have you thought of any more reasons why
    Alex is cute?"

"No."

"There must be other reasons. What are some
    more?"

"Only because he's silly."

And the next day when they were playing –

"Have you thought of any other reasons?"

"Yes. Right now. Because he talks funny."

This is the serious Amy. She had trouble with these questions. I think the format wasn't to her liking, she thought she was being interviewed. She was, actually. I wanted to see if she had anything to say about all this cuteness going on around our house. Usually, she has tons to say about her little brother and all you have to do is get her started.

Here's the real Amy –

> "We saw Caleigh's mom, and do you know what Alex said? This is sooooo funny. I will tell you. He said 'Hello Caleigh's mom'."

Here she is again. It was away past their bedtime. I don't know why. They were playing on the big bed in our room, and I heard Amy say –

> "I just love you so much I can't even stop laughing."

Don't stop laughing Amy, don't ever stop. It's so much fun to listen to Amy laugh when Alex is being funny. She laughs so hard!

And what does Alex think of Amy these days?

Poor Amy. She has a brother who is easily distracted, and that interferes with his expression of feelings for his sister. For instance, one night recently, I heard tons of laughter and Amy came running –

> "Quick Daddy, pick me up. Alex is after me, he's coming to get me, he's going to cut my hair, quick Daddy…."

I picked her up really fast. Then I looked down the hall for Alex but there was no sign of him. I hung on tightly, something was up. Where was he?

> "Well Daddy, if we wait long enough…."

We waited. Amy, what is it that happens if we wait long enough? We waited some more.

> "Daddy, let's go look for him."

And we found him, pouring bath crystals all over the bathroom floor. I'd have to do something about that.

Did you notice Amy's steady lessening of concern with a comment every few seconds as Alex continued to not show up? It was a fun game in spite of her initial protest. Then there was the suddenness and completeness of Alex's caving in to his distraction. I noticed that too. And it wasn't as if he was giving up on something he didn't enjoy – he loves chasing Amy, he does it all the time. I enjoyed their varying interest in the game. Not the bath crystals on the floor though, what a mess. I picked them up and threw them in the bathtub just ahead of the kids, it was bath time again.

One evening, Alex was very generous to Amy. She told me all about it.

"Do you know what? Alex gave me a balloon, a marble, a cup, a sticker, and a turtle."

That's a lot! Then she added, right away –

"Guess what. He gave me the turtle and the cup last."

She'd just about had enough.

"I'm getting full of toys from Alex. He wants to give me one more toy."

She said all of this with hardly a pause from beginning to end. If I'd wanted to say something, I'd have had to be quick. Then Alex came into the room. She said three more things, and this time, there was no way I could slip in a word edgewise. She said –

"I hope you don't give me another thing."

Followed immediately – with the same tone of voice – by –

"I hope you don't give me another thing."

And then she finished –

"Would you give me another thing?"

Amy enjoyed the attention, and was reluctant to let go even after Alex apparently lost interest. He was distracted. He thinks that Amy is okay until something else comes along.

*   *   *   *   *

Yes, usually they get along just fine. Sometimes though, if that "something else" doesn't come along quite soon enough, their behaviour is apt to become a little antagonistic for a short while before moving right into sibling rivalry. This is something I know all about – a long, long time ago, I was a sibling. You get over it.

Amy and Alex need to get over it. I can hardly wait. It's rather annoying and rather regular as well. So far, it hasn't progressed too much past getting in the last word, and there are numerous little rivalries. One senses that bigger ones can't be far off.

Alex tries so hard to be as big as Amy, as good, as smart, as funny as Amy, as everything else as Amy. He tries so hard not to let her get ahead at all. Look at what he said one night at dinnertime. Amy began –

> "Do you know what helps me eat all my dinners? I take a drink first. It makes me hungry."

> "And I do that too."

> "Take a drink first?"

> "It makes me hungry and my dinner is all gone."

> "It doesn't make your dinner all gone."

Early sibling rivalry, a little quarrel in the making here. Four-year-old Amy thinks her young brother is talking through his hat. Moreover, he needs to know that.

The rivalry even extends to phone calls. Amy was talking to Madzy, and then passed the phone to Alex, who told Madzy –

> "I like carrots."

Amy grabbed the phone back.

> "I like carrots too."

Alex grabbed the phone back.

> "I like carrots STILL."

I'd just heard a juvenile approach to getting in the last word. Equally juvenile, the truth of the matter is that neither one of them likes carrots very much. They both should have a long drink before sitting down to carrots, that's for sure.

The other night, it was approaching bedtime and I said to Alex, musically I might add –

> "Brush, brush, brush, brush, all your little teeth."

Alex said –

"My teeth are big."

Amy said –

"Mine are bigger."

And Alex concluded –

"Me too."

Wasn't that ridiculous? I know, I know – I'm adult. Alex just wanted to have the last word again.

Rachel was coming for a visit with her younger sister Shannon. Amy and Alex had some candy to share, and Amy said –

"If Rachel wants one, I'm going to give her one."

Alex had to respond to that, of course he did, so he said –

"And if Shannon wants *two*, I'm going to give her one."

I thought he would have responded to the second part of what Amy said, not the first part. Wouldn't you have thought that? Signs of early sibling rivalry are popping up everywhere, but Alex has no rival when it comes to responding to the wrong part of what someone says. All he has is enthusiasm. When he was wondering where the store was where Grandma bought him some pajamas, I suggested to him –

"Next time you see her, ask her where she bought them."

What a great idea, thought Alex. So he said eagerly –

"Maybe next time, I WILL see her."

And on it goes.

Amy had just learned a new little song and she sang it in the car. She and Alex then had a few words. Alex said –

"I like that song Amy."

"Would you like to hear it again?"

"No."

What's the message? It depends on who you ask. Ask Dad: "Alex isn't three yet." Amy's viewpoint? "Alex's social skills need sprucing up." Or, if you were to ask Alex – "How to set up your 'No's' for maximum effect."

Amy doesn't like Alex whenever he does his "Amy-thumb-sucking-hair-twirling" imitation. He'll put a thumb in his mouth, and twirl his hair with the other, or "put a ponytail in it" as he says. This is exactly what Amy used to do, but never does anymore. For his own personal needs, he has a soother, so of course he only does this when Amy is present. Amy thinks it's all wrong. She's sensitive, and it showed one day when she and I were playing with her dolls.

Well yes – she and I. We were. Earlier, she had asked me if I would and I said yes. So my doll was Emily and I was trying to find her little thumb so I could pull it through her little sleeve but was having difficulty. I asked Amy –

> "You don't suppose she sucks her thumb and she sucked it right
> off her hand?"

> "She doesn't suck even her thumb anymore. She sucks nothing.
> She only sucks drinks."

She sounded a little irritated, and I suspect Alex's imitating behaviour was largely to blame.

One time, Amy wanted to get dressed all by herself. She did so very slowly and I was a bit impatient. I don't remember just what I said, but her reply was very clear –

> "DON'T HELP ME!"

> "Okay, okay. I won't help you."

Alex, ever-so-helpful, looked up at me, and quietly and very slyly said –

> "Help her."

There's a pattern here, isn't there. Alex has an attitude. Here it is. A few days ago, their playing together was becoming more and more physical, and I was sure Amy soon would be in tears. It was time to speak up –

> "Alex, Alex! Don't be so rough with Amy."

"But she's *my* sister!"

What an attitude. Ownership.

He thinks he can be rough with his sister whenever he wants. She may be *his* sister, but as well, Alex is *her* brother. I suppose that means she can take a swipe at him too. Whenever she wants, fair's fair. Things could get out of hand. Mom and dad need to stay attuned when roughhousing changes from play to something else.

It can be hard, one can't have an eye on them all the time. Lynn was cooking something this morning when there was a commotion elsewhere in the house. The kids had been playing well together, but now what. She was on her way to find out when Alex ran into the kitchen –

"Mommy! Mommy!"

"What's the matter sweetheart?"

"We have a problem! We have a problem with Amy! She hurt her
teeth on my head."

Now doesn't this create an interesting picture? She bit him so hard that her teeth are sore. She owed it to him, it had been building for some time. He mimics her, he gets in the last word more often than she does, he sets up his "no's", and – wasn't he some sibling when he quietly asked me to help her? So she took a swipe at him and bit him on the head.

In fact, they bumped heads, that's all. Her bump was near her mouth. Amy can't get the best even when it's an accident.

We're going home soon, and a change in the scenery is certain to induce a positive change in their dynamics. It isn't? Well, failing that, school begins in three or four weeks: a forced separation. No? Okay, okay, another year or two won't be too bad, we can handle it. HOW MANY YEARS?

PART 3

BACK HOME BEFORE SCHOOL

- 15 -

Summer excitement and fall routines

Around the second week of August, we moved back to Ottawa. Our vacation time was spent and the back-and-forth driving was beginning to wear.

The days are cooler now. Soon the autumn colours will be upon us and we'll be looking under the stairs for a rake. Piles of leaves will beckon – or maybe just one big pile for everyone. It's a time of energy and anticipation. Jane's daycare will reopen soon, and it won't be long before "I went to school" will be the right answer again.

So we're home from the cottage and in many ways, that's nice. We'll miss the jumps in the lake and a couple of excited faces bobbing along, and all the splashing and red and green water wings and blond hair shining wet in the summer evening sunshine. And we'll miss the smell of soggy dogs and dinnertime barbecues. We'll miss the loons at night. We'll miss the cottage a lot, but it's good to retrench and re-establish routines. There's an element of security in this, a little order restored to our busy lives.

For the kids though, it's non-routine as usual. There's just too much excitement every day. And as for security and order, if ever anyone needs that stuff, Dad or Mom will look after it.

Conversations with a four-year-old

Amy woke up quickly the morning we moved back. She hadn't seen her cousins for a long time and going home was going to be great.

"Hi Amy! Good morning."

"Good morning, Mommy's getting Alex dressed."

"I see you're all dressed yourself."

"No, Mommy helped me get dressed. Today's going to be an excited one!"

It already was. And we filled the car with boxes, bags, dogs and kids, and home we went.

* * * * *

So it was back to Ottawa, about three weeks before Alex's birthday as I recall. The days back home were as fun as the summer days at the cottage, and I enjoyed the two of them immensely. It was still my turn to hang around with little kids! More notes, many more vignettes ahead – our train rolled gently down the track, clickety-clack.

Two years ago in August, she was four-and-a-half and he was almost three. Alex could hardly wait to be three. It was just before his birthday when he told me one day that he'd like to steal a car. I was glad he told me. That, and other pronouncements, suggested that with his growing comprehension, it was time for reprimanding and correcting. My rambunctious son needed some discipline. So we talked about stealing cars, and Alex became better by the day at choosing words professing innocence. But the emphasis continued to rest right where it should: solidly on play. That's a child's prerogative and something to be pursued earnestly. They both did, and there was play every day those last three weeks of summer. Amy's play was scattered. Secrets were fun, they were special. Usually, they weren't so secret either, though she and Rachel shared one that no one will ever know, guaranteed. Clowns were a big part of her happy play too – games by day and dreams by night. Our train ride ended as summer turned to fall; Alex's birthday was the last stop.

Have you enjoyed your trip so far? I hope you've been reminded of other little ones, or at least of how you felt when you knew little ones at some point in your life. I'm always reminded of Amy and Alex when I see others. There is so much commonality, aspects like appearance, behaviour, learning, expression. Nowadays, I'm always happy if I can stop awhile and enjoy the magic of a two-year-old again. If a three- or a four-year-old happens to be along as well, that's even better.

It was a wonderful summer. I miss my impetuous two-year-old boy.

*   *   *   *   *

One night, very soon after we were back, I went into Alex's room. All was quiet and I was sure he was asleep. He was lying on his back looking angelic actually, sharply in contrast to a few minutes earlier when he still was roaring. His eyes were closed, and quietly, I leaned over and kissed him. Immediately he sat up and grabbed me. SPLAT – right on the cheek. And just as quickly, PLOP – back down in bed, eyes still closed. That was a noisy goodnight kiss. He was playing possum.

Gentleboy

Usually though, it's more peaceful as sleep approaches. A night or two later, I lay down with him for a few minutes but we weren't talking. For some forgotten reason, we were at odds with each other. I was tired, I suspect I'd been a bit cross with his persistence or maybe something specific he'd said or done. When I told him I was going, he put his arms around me and hugged me – still no words, just a hug. It was quiet and tight, it was a very warm moment. Later I said to Lynn, "The lad knows what hugs are about." What a gentle boy.

Grandpa came over one day and he said this to Alex –

"You're my little prince."

"No."

"You're my little prince and Amy's my little princess."

"No. I'm not."

Stubborn, isn't he. I offered –

"You're his grandson, aren't you Alex."

"I'm his little grandson. And Amy's his little grandgirl."

Gentle. Right Grandpa? Wasn't that a nice thing Alex just said? A grandson and a grandgirl – how about that, lucky man. A day or two later, he said to me –

"I wanted you to play with my beads."

"Oh I don't play with beads anymore. I used to play with beads
     when I was a little boy like you."

"But now you're not a little boy anymore, you're a big daddy. I
     love you Daddy."

Very gentle.

At least I thought so. Sometimes, I've wondered if "gentleboy" might be a word that should be in a dictionary. Do the attributes that allow one to call a "man" a "gentleman" relate only to one having grown old enough to no longer be thought of as a boy? No, it's the behaviour, the decorum of a man that qualifies him. Boys behave, and they have decorum too. So why can't there be "gentleboy"?

Michael visited again. He's three or four years older than Alex. The two of them were off playing in another part of the house and everything was quiet. All of a sudden, Alex came running up to me and shouted –

"Daddy! Michael just used a bad word. He said, 'STUPID'!"

The bad one was separated from the rest of his words, and clearly emphasized. Then, having apprised me of this, he ran back to Michael and all was quiet again. A few moments later, I heard from afar –

"Daddy! If Michael's going to say 'Stupid', I'm going to say, 'BUTTHEAD'!"

No, there's just no place for "gentleboy" and further deliberation on the matter is pointless. I shouldn't talk about decorum either because it's evident only on occasion. He's going to be a boy for a good while yet, and then comes adolescence.

*   *   *   *   *

Alex learned a new word: "butthead". I don't think he has a clue what it means. That's okay, I don't either. He thinks it's a bad word, but it's all right to use it if Michael is going to go around saying "stupid". By the way little boy, what does "stupid" mean? And why did Michael say that anyway?

So many new words, so much learning – where does it all come from? Michael goes home today, who's next? Back to Mom and Dad?

You make up some of it and that's fun. The social element of a small family tends to be insular when children come along. Made-up words are fine and work well. "Gentleboy" will never make it to a dictionary, but it's still reserved for Alex, disarming little fellow that he is from time to time. We love calling our big dog "Gagawagger", and we do that almost as often as we call him "Scott". If we don't have time for "Gagawagger", he gets "Big". Alex came up with "grandgirl", but that's only his latest. He invents words regularly. It's a little-kid behaviour trait, isn't it.

Side-door language

Then there's the mystery element in your little one's vocabulary growth. Mom guards the front door, dad guards the back, but there's no one to watch at the side door. So in come words, expressions, new ways of behaving – all with question marks regarding their origin, and in ever-increasing numbers.

The kid goes to preschool, watches television, goes to the park, makes new friends, learns to use words rather than nodding when hanging on to a phone, and so on. So now and again, a word comes forth that simply hasn't before. One notices. Often, you wish you could have been there – wherever – when it was first learned.

One day, "love bug" came in the side door. The four of us were in the kitchen when Madzy dropped by for a visit. Madzy has a very distinctive laugh, and when she laughs, she gets us all going. We were laughing a lot! Amy and Lynn had been bandying about the phrase "wicked woman" for a day or two. There had been accusations back and forth. Lynn said –

"Do you know what Madzy? Amy's a wicked woman."

Alex, being naturally imitative, said –

"Amy's a wicked woman."

Then it was Amy's turn to add something and she said –

"I love you Madzy."

She changed the subject! How clever. Mom said –

"Oh Amy, that's really, really a nice thing to say. You couldn't possibly be a wicked woman."

"I'm not, I'm a love bug."

And there's the side-door language. She'd never said "love bug" before, not to us anyway, and we had no idea where she learned it. Oh well, we missed that one. Alex imitated again, with a small alteration probably just to get attention. He said –

"She's a love love."

We tried to correct Alex, but he thought it was hilarious to be a "love love". Amy thought so too. Love love it is, and the word-learning goes on. Grandgirl and gentleboy, love bug and love love. Wicked woman. No, that's over. A day or so later, I heard Amy remark –

"I'm not a wicked woman, I'm a princess woman."

Things are always changing around our house and from one day to another, you never know what Amy is.

Rated – PG

Where does it all come from? Mostly parents of course. "Silly" is a word we're all using these days.

Alex was smiling and quietly playing with something. Amy was curious and took a look. Then she turned to me and whispered with a big behind-his-back smile of her own –

"I don't know what he's up to."

Me neither. I asked him –

"Alex, what are you up to?"

"I'M UP TO A SILLY THING."

He said this loudly, brashly – even proudly – but not at all in a way that detracted him from his sense of purpose. So, I guess he was up to a silly thing, and he carried on just as quietly, maybe smiling even a little more. He often talks about doing "things".

"That's what I'm going to do. I'm going to do some things for a
little bit."

I think he says this when he doesn't know what he's going to do, or maybe he just doesn't know the words to describe what he's going to do. Or maybe he knows he shouldn't be doing it. Anyway, now he's learned the word "silly" and he can be more specific.

It was likely a toy that he had, likely a non-breakable. I usually notice and respond when breakables are the object of his "silly thing" activity. It hasn't always been this way, but one learns.

Here's something else I've learned: If dad likes the word enough, the kid will use it. Now isn't that a unique observation. This is the PG element, parental guidance – front- and back-door learning. Almost everything comes in this way in the early stages, and there shouldn't be very many surprises.

"Silly" has long been a favourite word of mine. It's like "Big much little bit" in that it's a more adult word than most. One needs perspective. Alex may have begun using the word, but his usage is not quite right yet. A few days ago, all evening long he described his sister as an "Amy silly".

Whenever he referred to her, that's what she was, and he referred to her much more than usual.

Amy's understanding is marginally better –

"He said I said he could bite me. I didn't say that. He's just a silly old boy."

Conversations with a four-year-old

The tap in the bathroom sink was dripping, and when Amy noticed this, she didn't turn it off. Of course not –

"See, I can feel the water when I push my finger up the tap where it's coming out."

"Be careful you don't spray it all over the place."

"Look, I can feel it."

"I know. I used to do that when I was a little boy. But be careful."

"And did your daddy say 'Don't do that'?"

Amy I don't remember, how would I remember that. I said nothing as I shut off the tap.

A parent is in a bit of a quandary here: non-PG learning this time. It includes all the little things that one needs to learn as a young child, but that one's parents likely aren't going to be teaching – like stopping a dripping tap with your finger, or playing with your gum. Putting down your spoon and drinking the rest of the milk in your cereal bowl is another. There are several, so how is a parent supposed to make sure the kid learns them all?

"Don't blow bubbles in your glass Alex!"

We don't have to worry about that one. He's learned it. But he hasn't learned he's not supposed to do it when Dad or Mom is watching. We're still working on that.

I'm much more comfortable with the PG stuff. It starts simple, and a parent guides and fine-tunes the growth, all in due course. In the meantime, it's a little bit of magic and it's there to be enjoyed. It's so easy to do this; it's beautiful and so much fun. "Enjoying" is a parenting essential when you're messing about with one of these little ones. Or two or three. Absolutely, there should be an exam.

> "That's what Blacks Eyes said. She said we can't go to the cottage anymore. We have to stay at home and sleep. Blacks Eyes is a silly doll."

More Alex and Blacks Eyes

Alex loves his doll Blacks Eyes, of that there is no doubt. She has played a very large role in his young life. I think the name he gave her is wonderful. It has character. It's an unusual name, one you don't hear very often.

Then one day, very suddenly, Alex called her "Black Eyes" instead. I had no idea why he did this. When he continued with this variation, I became concerned. It was no mistake. I wasn't upset, but I was curious why it happened and would I be able to change it back. I wanted to, and trying might be fun. As it turned out, as fun as it was, it was quite trying too. It sure was a challenge. We had many exchanges over the two or three weeks before school and here are some of them. Our game began.

I approached the issue quietly and politely. I suggested that since he changed his doll's name, maybe I could change his. I gave him a few options.

"Could I call you….Jujube?"

"No."

"Could I call you Bebop?"

"No."

"Peter?"

"No."

"Alex?"

"I'm already Alex. I'm Christopher Alexander Cook, so you don't
    need to call me another Alex."

"Can I call you Blacks Eyes?"

"No."

"Can I call you Black Eyes?"

"Black Eyes?"

"Yes."

"No. You can call me ChristopherAlexanderCook."

He ran his three names together, saying them very quickly. He's always
liked his name very much. That's fine, I'll call him that. He didn't even
nibble when I offered Blacks Eyes or Black Eyes as possibilities. I was
hoping for some insight as to why the change. I kept wondering about that.
Who would have put him up to it, was it one of his cousins from
downstairs? It certainly wasn't Lynn or Amy, nor did they have any idea
who it might have been.

I continued with some more gentle nudging. I told him I really liked the
name "Peter". Would that be okay?

"No, me Alex."

I reminded him how he used to always call her Blacks Eyes, how it was he
who had named her that, how I'd always liked the name so much. He
said –

"Me used to know how to call her that, but me don't know how
    anymore."

He doesn't know how? How could he not know how! I approached my
concern more directly –

"Alex. I want you to start calling her 'Blacks Eyes' again."

"When I be a baby again."

Well I'm not going to wait for that. I pushed, I told him the same thing
again. This time he replied –

"Soon me will. Me call her that in the morning. But not when she sleeps."

Not in the morning either, I was listening. He was really digging in, and I still had no idea why. Was it a babysitter? Was it Madzy? Very reluctantly, I was about to concede when something happened.

We went back to the cottage one weekend in late August, and I did the packing. When we arrived, Lynn asked if I'd brought Blacks Eyes. Alex must have thought she had been left at home because when I told Lynn which bag she was in, he said loudly and clearly –

"BLACKS EYES IS HERE?"

AT LAST! Or did he just slip up. He slipped up. I couldn't get him to do it again, nor to admit he'd even done it in the first place. But he had, I was certain of it, and I had new hope.

I decided to try an emotional approach. I begged him. I implored him to call her "Blacks Eyes" and I put all my weight behind my urging. He just looked at me and said nothing. I begged him some more – no more gentle nudging, that's for sure. Finally he said, very quietly –

"I can't say that noise."

"That noise"! The beautiful name "Blacks Eyes" is now "That noise"? Alex, how rude! How can you talk to your father that way! Shame on you!

So much for the emotional approach.

It was time to reason with the lad. I carefully explained to him how if he can change Blacks Eyes to Black Eyes, we can change Alex to Peter. The one follows from the other, the logic is perfect, isn't it. Even a two-year-old can understand this. And I told him that we *would* change his name too. No doubt about it.

I was feeling smug. I was sure I had him and I'd be hearing "Blacks Eyes" again in no time. How could he possibly wiggle out of this one?

He had an unusually serious demeanor, he looked very disconsolate. Why, I thought he might even cry. Then sadly, softly, he said –

"You can call me Peter."

That's how. He wiggled out. Help.

Amy tried to help –

"Alex, say 'black'."

"Black."

"Say 'sighs'."

"Sighs."

"There. Now say 'Black sighs'."

"BLACK EYES!"

Thanks for trying Amy. Nice to see our family working together to help Alex with his problem. Lynn, do you have any ideas?

"Whose problem?"

Then one evening, as quickly as it started, it was over. It was bedtime and there had already been several callbacks. Alex had more to say though –

"Daddy, my doll keeps waking me up."

I was at the point of ignoring him because sleep was very close at hand. However, his doll is Blacks Eyes and he hadn't been paying her much attention lately. I thought maybe we could play another round in our little game. So I went to him and said –

"Well you can ask her nicely to be quiet."

"Be quiet."

"Maybe you should say 'please'."

"Please be quiet."

"Call her nicely by her right name."

"Please be quiet...."

"Say her name."

"No, I want you to do it."

"You do it, she's your doll."

"Please be quiet, Black Eyes."

"No. Her *right* name. Blacks Eyes."

"Please be quiet Blacks Eyes. Hey. I know her right name, I'm going to tell Amy."

Blacks Eyes continued to make noise and keep him awake. He called me back a couple of times to tell me that. As well, he kissed her on the lips and when he did fall asleep, he was hugging her. It was the first time in a long while he'd done this.

And yet another beautiful day with Alex and Blacks Eyes was over. I wonder how many more there will be. Some day, he'll fall asleep for the last time with his arm around his noisy little friend; morning will come and he'll not awaken her. That will be sad – our three will be two again. I know, that was our intent, but back then Blacks Eyes was simply unimaginable. I hope that sad day is far away.

With the two of them sleeping tightly together, it's time to put our game to rest. I love Alex's comment, "Hey. I know her right name". His words were those of genuine enlightenment, he thought he had learned something entirely new. I'm grateful about that. I'm happy it ended as it did because long after that sad day down the road, I'll still remember the doll named Blacks Eyes. That's the one my son loved so much when he was a very little boy. I'll always remember that.

*　　*　　*　　*　　*

So. His silly doll thinks we should stay home and sleep. At least that's what Alex told us she said. Very silly, I'LL say. We went anyway. One weekend late in August, and whether she wanted to or not, Blacks Eyes came along too. I made sure of that.

Yes, I do like the word "silly". I like its sound, I like what it means: "dazed, goofy, frivolous" by one definition. I like to use it, and I really like to hear Amy and Alex use it.

"Guys" is another word with a sound that catches my ear regularly. Kaitlyn used it all the time this summer at the cottage. She didn't know many words because she just turned two in June, but this one she knew well. When the four of them were outside going somewhere, she would always be bringing up the rear and she'd holler, "Wait for me guys." And they'd be outside going somewhere almost every day. We heard this many, many times. I like the word – it sounds a bit odd when my mind lingers on it. I seldom use it myself though, and I never heard my kids use it at all until one night at bedtime just after we were home from our trip to Tweed in July.

The day had been very playful, more than usual, and we were all a little late going to bed. Eventually, Amy climbed into the top bunk and I lay down with Alex. I must have taken too long saying goodnight to him, or so thought Amy. She was very weary and she told me she wanted SOON a hug and a kiss. She went on with a quiet, serious tone of voice –

"Every night when I go to bed, I make sure I give you guys hugs
and kisses."

She certainly caught my attention with that. I don't think I'd ever heard her refer to Lynn and me as "you guys". I stood up right away. She propped herself up, and as she gave me one of each, I was struck by the expression on her tired face. It was one of dutiful resignation and complete boredom. Cute though. And she was off to sleep in a moment.

I started using the word more myself around then, I even had a little joke with the two of them. One Friday night when we were all a bit tired, the kids were in bed, and I said –

"Now you guys have a good sleep, and don't forget, when you
wake up in the morning, there's one thing I want you to do
before anything else. Go back to sleep."

I thought this was funny, and so did they. It certainly fitted my wishing for a little extra sleep Saturday morning at the end of the week. I found myself saying something along these lines regularly for awhile. Then last Friday evening, back home in Ottawa, I said –

"Guys, you know what? It's the weekend and we're going to have a
really good time. Tomorrow morning, there's something I want

you to do right away when you wake up. Do you know what it is?"

"Go back to sleep."

They replied in unison – without a laugh, no chuckle, not even a tired smile. It was a good joke once upon a time, but no longer. I'll have to look for something else to humour me in my tiredness.

Alex likes "guys" too now. Just the other night, I came home from work and heard him on the stairs. He said, "Hi Daddy." I asked, "Who is it?" He filled me in –

"It's the guy who had Blacks Eyes, it's Alex, here I am."

By the way, the word's out – it was Grandpa! Kristen told me. She overheard him one day. Grandpa is the one who told Alex that "Blacks Eyes" is wrong. Alex loves his Grandpa indeed, so when he suggested dropping the "s" from "Blacks", this must be important.

I should have known, Grandpa was a teacher in his heyday.

- 17 -

"Silly", "guys", and there's one more – another word I just love. I love its sound and its happy connotations. I sat down at the kitchen table and turned to Alex –

"So, what did you do today?"

This was suppertime, not bedtime, so I thought I might hear something different. I did –

"Play."

That's the word! It's something a little kid should do just as often as possible; there will never be a better time – good boy Alex. What a good word.

Prelude to play

There's no end to the play going on at our house these days. Amy says that first you have to prepare yourself. I had no idea. The two of them were outside in the yard screaming and screaming when Amy decided her dad might want to know why the racket. In she came and said –

"Do you know why we're screaming?"

"No. Tell me."

"In case we hurt ourselves."

Okay, well done. The preparations are finished and you're all set for hurting yourselves. Enough screaming now, go and play like you're supposed to play.

I'm more used to working, not screaming, as a prelude to playing. I hardly ever scream. One time, Amy worked before play – very thoroughly. It was back in April only a few days after she turned four. It was beautiful to watch her and listen to her that sunny afternoon.

It had snowed and there was some shoveling to be done. Lynn was working with one shovel, Amy had another which was smaller and her own. She didn't move too much anywhere but she applied herself diligently, talking all the time about where each shovelful goes. This one goes here, this one there. This went on for quite a while. Very seriously, intently, and very imitatively, she shoveled and shoveled. Then she stopped.

"Would you like me to shovel some more or play in the snow?"

"I'd like you to play in the snow."

She began immediately. Very seriously, intently – and not at all like her mother – she played and played and played. She carried on just like a little kid, just the way she's supposed to carry on.

Yes, it was a warm summer day in August and their screaming had ended. Amy was through telling me about it too, and it was outside again to play. But almost right away, Alex charged back into the house. Not to talk about more screaming, or maybe a little work – he had to go to the bathroom. That's the only prelude that matters to him.

It was just a quick visit, and he didn't want to take off his shoes. He held one foot up right in front of me and said –

"If you see, they won't be dirty. See?"

I saw, they weren't dirty. I said –

"That's fine Alex."

"They're dirty on the inside."

Before I could say anything else, off he went, intended course of action unchanged and ready at last for his summertime play. It was not the time to look inside his shoes. Later when we took them off, it would be up to us to remember what he just said. Not his problem, they filled up while he was playing. Now there will come a point. I'm not going to wait until winter. Maybe next week I'll talk to him about the inside of his shoes, maybe the week after, maybe….

Sometime when he's not playing – that's when I'll talk to him. "Play" is a child's word, a happy, fun-sounding word. We'll talk about taking sand out of his shoes when his play is done.

*   *   *   *   *

Conversations with a four-year-old

We've been back in Ottawa for a week now, and Rachel is coming for a visit with her family. Amy can show Rachel her ring. She went to a birthday party and came home with a pencil and a ring with a clown's face on it.

"Look what I got."

"That's really nice. Did everyone get
   something?"

"Yes. Everyone got the same thing. Even I did."

She loves her clown ring and plays with it a lot. Standing near the window waiting for her friend, she looked to be deep in thought.

"What are you thinking about Amy?"

"I'm thinking about maybe Rachel and
   Shannon and I can play in the backyard."

"Sure you can, it's going to be a nice
   evening."

"Don't ever ask people what they're thinking
   because they might be busy thinking."

Amy thinks about thinking. She thinks about poems too. Last night, just before bedtime, she wanted to tell me her poem.

"Would you like to hear my poem? It's about
    lions and monkeys."

"Yes I would."

"Well, it's very long."

"Do you know all the words?"

"No. I don't. I need to think about it. You
    know, when I think I go like this."

She turned her head and looked sideways at me, very seriously, very pensively. Lions, monkeys, maybe giraffes, maybe tigers – she was thinking all right.

"Let me hear your poem."

"Well, it's pretty long."

"Good. I like long poems."

"It will take until morning. It's as long as the
    house."

A poem as long as the house? I don't think so. She must have been joking. Amy likes joking. She went on.

"Can I have some gum?"

"No, it's bedtime."

Lots of laughter – both of us. She was joking again.

"Have you ever seen anyone chew gum all night
    long in their sleep?"

"No, I haven't."

"Well, giants say they can do whatever they
    want, so they could do that if they wanted
    to."

So. Giants can chew gum. I didn't know that.

"I have lots of funny jokes, don't I."

"You sure do."

"But some of them are breakable."

"Breakable? What do you mean?"

"Sometimes, I don't know what to say. That
means they're breakable."

"And if they break, you always fix them."

"You're my favourite dad I ever had, heh heh,
wasn't that a funny word?"

Amy is not always sure of herself when she mixes words with feelings. The "heh heh" means that if it doesn't make much sense, it must be a joke. Happily she climbed into bed, we said goodnight, and as I left and closed the door quietly, I thought to myself how much I like being her favourite dad.

I really enjoyed my conversation with my little four-year-old last night, and here we are chatting again waiting for Rachel.

"Amy, where's Alex? Our friends will be here
soon, it's beautiful outside."

No sign of our friends, no sign of Alex either. He's her favourite brother but he doesn't care. Amy was thinking again, and while we waited she said –

"Do you know what? I once told Alex a
funny story that made him so happy that
he fell asleep and had a bad dream."

"You did? You told Alex a story that was so
funny that he became really happy and fell
asleep right away and had a bad dream?"

"Uh huh."

I used to talk to Amy about her dreams, and she told me that she always dreamed about clowns. I asked her what her dreams are about now, and she said –

"I don't know about what because the dream
        makes it up. That's what the clown says,
        not me."

So, clown dreams continue.

Oh! There's a knock on the door. It's Rachel!

"Hi Amy."

Good friends, happy birthdays, long poems, noisy laughter, funny jokes, funny stories, clown rings and dreams – Amy is a happy girl. And she likes to play and play and play. There they go!

"Go play in the backyard you two! Don't
        forget Shannon! And what about Alex, here
        he comes...."

*   *   *   *   *

Alex and the police

This was the big, big game in Alex's summertime play. It began at the cottage in early August and continued right up to his birthday.

The beginning ....

Alex didn't like something that Kaitlyn was doing, and he said very loudly –

"Tell somebody to call the police."

We heard him in the next room above the commotion of the four of them playing together. Then we heard, less loudly, almost a whisper –

"The police are going to come and get you."

.... the play, ...

It was very common for the next three or four weeks to hear Alex say something like –

"Hello? Get me the police. Come and get Amy. She's being bad."

He'd often be holding a yellow toy phone up to his ear when he said this. What a good thing it is that he doesn't know how to phone the police for real. He played his game day after day, with occasional variations such as his warning to Kaitlyn. Amy jumped in at one point too, pretending to be on the phone and saying –

"Police? Could you come and get Alex? He's being bad and I don't know what to do with him. Okay? Goodbye."

I thought her words reflected well their 17-month age difference. Alex doesn't have time for that many words all at once.

.... the bizarre, ...

It gets interesting. Some would say, "healthy, young imaginations". Not me, this is beyond that.

Here's a variation I heard from Alex one morning. He looked right at me and said –

"The police are going to give you a ticket."

Healthy imagination so far. However, he then asked me earnestly if he could have the ticket. He wanted to play with it.

Another time, he and I were the only ones in the room. While I was reading, Alex played. He picked up his yellow phone and said –

"Hello police? Come and get Alex."

"Alex, why did you call the police to come and get you?"

"Well I was being bad."

I hadn't noticed. I wonder what he was doing.

Right after this, Amy came into the room and said to Alex with much enthusiasm –

"Sometime could you put me in jail?"

"Okay. Right now."

Bizarre. Once in the middle of their play, Amy wanted uppy because the police were coming for her. I didn't know what to do. Alex was the arresting officer. Do I harbour a fugitive, or do I turn my four-year-old daughter over to the not-so-long arm of the law? What to do, what to do....

.... the finale.

Grandma was babysitting. Jane's daycare wouldn't be opening for another week. I've no idea who, but someone had told Alex that 911 was a phone number he might want to try sometime. I'm sure it wasn't put to him quite that way, but it may as well have been.

Anyway, this was the morning he did it. And after Grandma was off the phone from explaining and apologizing, she turned to our little boy and said –

"Alex, don't ever call that number again! If you do, THE
   POLICE WILL COME!"

Well. Grandma, no. Please. Please don't tell me you said that. Did we not tell you about his little game, about his wanting the police....? Oh my.

18

August has been such a fun month. To use Amy's word, so many of the days have been excited ones. It's a beautiful age these two are sporting right now.

Going out the window

Every day, whether it's "excited" or not, when we're not at the cottage I take a bus downtown to work. The bus stop is a short block from our house and my morning departure goes something like this.

The kids are up, I say goodbye. As I'm leaving, Lynn asks, "Do you want to watch Daddy go out the window?" I go downstairs, outside, and turn around and wave on the way to the bus. Almost always, Alex and usually Amy are either in Mom's arms or standing on a chair by the window so they can see and wave back. It's very nice.

After awhile it became an old joke. Time after time Mom would say the same thing: "Do you want to watch Daddy go out the window?" And we'd smile. Always these words, and we'd never explain the ambiguity. We waited and waited for one of them to notice.

It happened in August. We'd only been home a day or two, so naturally our little game had been dormant. When we tried it again though, Alex said –

"When you go to work, Mommy tell me to watch you go out the window, but you need to go out the door."

And that was that.

I wonder if he saw humour in all of this like Lynn and I did. I wonder too if all along he really did think I'd go out the window when Mommy said, more or less, that's what I'd be doing. Maybe that's why I'd see him standing on the chair. It's not that he loves me, he just wanted to see a trick.

Maybe that's why. He had seen so many neat new things. He'd seen his first car, his first fireworks, he'd been kissed by a 70-pound dog without being hurt. From a distance, he'd seen his first airplane – why he'd believe almost anything.

He'd also seen his first magic show. He came along when we took Amy to a birthday party where there was a magician. We told him he might see a bunny pulled out of a hat. He could hardly wait to pat the bunny, but all else was lost on him. Not interested, bored, restless, that was Alex. How can a magician compete with an airplane.

Yes, he'd seen many airplanes, many hot air balloons too. That's it! Maybe he thought I'd climb out the window into a hot air balloon and float off towards the bus stop. I can see him now if I did do that. Would he be amazed? No. Lynn would be amazed. Amy would be absolutely startled and would call her friends to come and see. Alex? He'd hardly give me a second glance before turning to Mom and saying –

"When me be big, me go to work out the window just like Daddy."

Emulating Daddy

Just like Daddy. I'm not surprised, there aren't many role models for a two-year-old and to be very frank, I'm not bad at a lot of things. Alex liked the way I could stand in front of a toilet – I'm certainly fine with that one. He was quite boastful when he finally managed it. He was funny, he was so proud when he first did that. No more sitting.

One day, after Alex gave Danny a not-too-good brushing, I took the brush and said –

"Thanks Alex, now I'm going to give Danny a big brushing."

"Some day I'll be a big daddy and I can give her a big brushing.
    I'm going to be a big daddy for Halloween!"

Great idea, what a chance to emulate me! And I already have his costume.
Pants, shirts – I've a drawer full of sweaters. What will it be Alex? A
sweater? You'll be swamped!

The next morning he wanted to be a fireman, don't we all, and later on –

"I'm going to be a fireman AND a dad. Mixed up."

Alex loves Halloween. Amy does too. She's not mixed up though, not like
the boy. She's confident of all sorts of things and becoming more so all the
time. Furthermore, she doesn't emulate anybody if she can help it. Not
anymore.

Lynn and I know this, so we need to be very careful should our talk ever
turn to genetic hand-me-downs. You know, "Very well, now that you ask, I
have my grandmother's nose, my mother's eyes, and everyone says I've
inherited my dad's bad manners." Or some such. This can happen
sometimes when adults come together and children are nearby.

Lynn took Amy to her office one day and introduced her to Johanne, and
Johanne wasn't careful at all –

"Amy, that's pretty blond hair. Is that your daddy's or your
    mommy's?"

"IT'S MINE!"

"All right, I won't ask any more silly questions."

Lynn laughed when the little one said what she did. Amy had just heard
someone ask her, quite seriously so it seemed, whether she was wearing
her mom's hair, or was it her dad's hair on top of her head. These were her
only two choices and she wasn't too pleased with either of them. Well no
wonder, come on Johanne – no more silly questions.

*   *   *   *   *

There's a boy coming upstairs

Did you have difficulty imagining my going out the window and floating off to the bus stop? If you did, you're probably older than three. Then too, you're not familiar with the configuration of the neighbouring trees and roof lines, to say nothing of the odd telephone pole. Coming home from work is easier, so visualize this. It has to do with a very special greeting I received one evening.

When I show up, the dogs are down the front stairs in their basement "apartment". Their 8 x 8-foot room comes with a window, a soft old chair, and a bowl of water. Perfect. Jane's daycare on the first floor is open again and that's where the kids are. Lynn is still at work. We stagger our work hours so one of us can be home a little longer at each end of the day.

The first thing I do is bring up the dogs and take them around to the back yard. Then, it's up the outside stairs and inside for their dinner before we head off for our evening walk. The back door is at the end of a long hall. There's a window, a little one, but it's still quite dark. And there's a bench for sitting to put shoes on or off, or, just for sitting.

Danny often barks when I arrive, and one evening Amy heard her and said she'd meet me upstairs. Sure enough, when I came in, there she was on the bench by the door. I sat down right beside her. The bench is very small, so there was just enough room. We played with Danny and Scott and had some fun.

Then I heard a loud, definite voice from the front hall –

"THERE'S A BOY COMING UPSTAIRS."

The intention was that there'd be no doubt that the voice would be heard. In he came, down the hall, and after a few words, he climbed onto my lap. I looked over his shoulder and said –

"Where's the boy who came upstairs?"

Alex didn't hesitate. Immediately he leaned forward so I could clearly see his face when he turned towards me, which he then did, without a word, but with a huge, phony, ear-to-ear grin. He broke me up. They started back downstairs to Jane's when I was about to feed the dogs, but came running back together for a forgotten kiss and hug. What a wonderful few moments in the mostly dark on that little bench by the back door.

Jane's work

So he broke me up. Phony grins don't usually do that. A few days later, I turned the tables on him. I broke him up. I didn't mean to, but it happened nonetheless. We were discussing "work", and I put it in the context of "Jane's daycare". I said –

> "You know what Aunt Jane's work is, don't you? It's looking after you."

That's what broke him up. He laughed for a long time, and when he stopped, he said –

> "Noooo. She don't go to work."

So much for that. Further lessons on work will just have to wait. But the next time the little boy breaks me up – or at least says something or does something that makes me laugh – will hardly have to wait at all. He does it all the time.

*　　*　　*　　*　　*

There's lots and lots of laughter these days. And warmth. Here's one of those warm moments when you sit down and talk to your soon-to-be-three-year-old about nothing much. Mom began –

> "You're my baby."

> "No. I'm not."

> "Oh yeah. You're my big boy."

> "But I'm a little bit small."

> "That's right, of course you are."

> "I'm big, but I'm not big like you to drive the car."

I don't know what it is about cars and Alex. The other day he asked me about a few old keys on a key ring we had given him –

"Are these the right keys for driving the car?"

I said "No" and thought that since he'd guessed wrong, he'd then ask me what the keys were for. But he didn't. Instead, he asked –

"Where are the right keys?"

I don't think I'll tell him.

Touching and stealing

It was just a few days before his birthday. We were downtown shopping and walking through a rather crowded parking lot. While I was watching carefully for cars pulling out, Alex was preoccupied with the ones that weren't. He likes touching, and he'd touch each one he passed. He'd say "touch" every time. I thought this was cute until it occurred to me how dirty his fingers must be getting. I took his hand and that's when he said something that stopped me in my tracks.

"Could we steal a car some day, could we?"

What a question – Wow! I'd never even heard him say "steal" before! How does Dad deal with a question like this. I could say "No." That would do. Or I could elaborate: "I don't think so Alex, I'm not into that." Of course, he doesn't really want a car, he just wants to be in on stealing one. Maybe we could arrange a heist late some night around his birthday and return it the next day.

No, his question was in earnest and he deserved a serious answer. I spoke up with emphasis –

"NO! That would be very BAD! Do you know what it means to steal somebody's car?"

"WHAT?!"

If I raise my voice, you can be sure Alex will raise his. He's not easily humbled.

"It means you take something that's not yours. What if someone
     stole our car. How would we get home?"

Alex, Alex the philosopher that is, you know the one – the little kid, never
stuck for an answer – had quite an answer to that one –

"Well we could go home in the car that we steal."

His philosophy is going to put him in jail some day. Yes, quite an answer –
such deductive reasoning. Or did these words come out by accident? Hmm.
I only had to wait until the next day to find out.

We went to a craft show and Alex wanted to touch everything. I took him
aside while the other two went on ahead, and sat him on my lap and
explained about "breakables" and "responsibility" as best I could. I think
he understood, sort of. Off he went to catch up, but first he told me to keep
quiet. Then he told me not to follow. About half way, he turned around to
see if I was doing as I was told. I was. He shouted to me, "If you see me
touch anything, I'll come right back."

Now that's the kind of deductive reasoning one would expect of a two-
year-old. I'll keep my eyes open, my mouth shut, and if I see him touch
anything, he'll come right back.

It was an accident.

*   *   *   *   *

I can't tell you something

I wasn't long home from work one evening when Alex came up to me and
said –

"Well I can't tell you something."

Then he stood there looking at me.

I suppose if I had taken him at his word, I'd have gone right on with what I
was doing. There's something he can't tell me, he didn't, and that's that.
But he didn't want that. I responded –

"What is it that you can't tell me?"

"I can't tell it."

"Why not?"

"Kristen told me not to tell you or Mommy."

So Alex and Kristen have a secret, I respect that. Alex doesn't though. If this was really a secret, then it must be something special, and he wanted his daddy to know about it. He emulates me, remember? You're wonderful Alex.

I ignored what he actually said, and assumed that his "Well I can't tell you something" meant that he was really excited by what he was about to tell me. And he did, almost right away. It was rather innocuous. Kristen had put some make-up on his eyes, or some such.

Secrets are so much fun with little kids! Even the deepest ones just bubble out if you give them a chance.

Conversations with a four-year-old

"Daddy, I have a secret to tell you."

I picked her up and held her with her mouth right beside my ear because there were others in the room –

"Tell me Amy. Whisper. What's your secret?"

"I can't tell you."

"Yes you can, what is it?"

"That's my secret. 'I can't tell you'."

I put her down again, so much the wiser.

Another time, she was wanting to whisper "Pssst" loudly in my ear. This was a game she and Alex had been playing, and now it was my turn. She said from across the room –

"Do you want me to tell you a secret?"

"Sure."

She came over and cupped her mouth against my ear.

> "Okay. Once there was a little girl and she
> walked down the lane to the grocery store
> and she bought bananas and celery and
> oranges. Do you know what the orange's
> name was?"

"What?"

"PSSST."

Then she laughed while I tapped my head to see if my ear was still working.

One Saturday afternoon the four of us, and Rachel too, went to see a play. There was a concern. The last time we did this, Alex had been kicked out for making too much noise. What a bad boy he was. Not this time though, and when we were home again, I said to him –

> "Alex, you were very good at the play. You were
> so quiet."

Right then, Amy just had to say something –

> "We were good too. No. We weren't as good
> because we were whispering."

> "What were you whispering, is it a secret?"

Amy and Rachel both nodded yes, very seriously, because after all, it was a secret, and secrets are very, very important. Will this one bubble out? I sure do love it when my four-year-old has a secret and I could hardly wait to hear it. Then she said –

> "Do you know what? We can't tell because we
> don't remember."

Okay, okay. I'm not waiting to hear it. OKAY?

That was disappointing. But not too much.

*   *   *   *   *

Our train will be slowing down soon, Alex's birthday is just down the track. That's no secret – he mentions it almost every day. He's wondering about his presents and it's fun to talk about this with him.

"What would you like for your birthday?"

"An umbrella."

Okay, well we knew that actually.

"What else would you like?"

"A toy."

"What kind of toy?"

"Yellow."

While Dad was picturing a lad of few words and definite tastes, his more practical mom was saying, "He'll be easy to shop for, he hasn't a clue what he wants." So we've a bit of shopping ahead, and all we have to do is find the nearest toy store and ask where the department with "yellow" is.

I hope you've booked your room and can stay a few days. It looks like another extended birthday party coming up and you're invited. It's only a whistle stop away.

19

When Alex is bad

Yes, Alex was a bad boy that first time at the theatre. Was he ever. We were in the second row of the balcony and he began to behave like a wild boy about half way through the first Act. He and I had to leave, that's for sure.

At home where it's quieter and Alex is bad and about to be reprimanded, he tries to preempt the scolding by saying –

"I'm good. I am. I am."

He says it slowly and his intonation is wonderful. It's very musical – he rolls the "o's" and "a's". And his words are encased in that "how-can-you-doubt-me" look of his, and they're followed by a quiet that suggests all the confidence in the world that what he just said – and deliberately repeated – is irrefutable. He doesn't have to say anything else, and what's more, there's nothing that could possibly be said to him that would be relevant. That's it, end of story.

One speaks generally of the sweet innocence of childhood. Is this what Alex is talking about? He's sweet, he's a child. Very thoroughly he says he's innocent, so maybe it is. You might be wondering if he gets away with it. Let me ask you this. How would you respond to a little boy, less than three, so seriously intent on bending an adult viewpoint to his own end? Of course he gets away with it. Sometimes anyway, so to him it's worth a try.

Have you bought your present? Maybe you don't think he deserves one. You still have time though because we're not quite there. His party doesn't begin until Wednesday. Don't get him a small plastic tiger, we just bought him one – yellow. Here's a suggestion. Softly and sweetly, with a very warm smile, he asked me just the other day –

"Daddy, when are you going to buy me a two-piece bathing suit?"

We're not. *We're* not going to be buying him one. So think about it.

*   *   *   *   *

His learning about two-piece bathing suits is coming right along. He didn't even know there was such a thing until he saw Aunt Laurie in Tweed. Now he's seen a few, he knows what they're called, he thinks they look good on people, and he wants one for himself. Amy has one, so why not. He's learned quite a bit about two-piece bathing suits, hasn't he.

And all the while Alex is learning, Amy becomes more and more loving.

Conversations with a four-year-old

Wonderful loving – it's there all the time with little kids. It feels so good, even before they know the words. Amy didn't know them that time she said "Bye bye" to me when she was having a bath, but I felt love and it was wonderful. Then they learn the words and use them all the time, never too much though. Here's Amy talking to me this morning –

> "I love Mommy so much in the world. I love Daddy so much in the world. I love Alex so much in the world. I love Scott and Danny so much in the world, them are good friends aren't they."

> "Yes they are. Did you say Alex?"

> "Yes. I love Alex so much in the world. Did you write that down?"

> "Yes I did."

Caught again. Well what could I say? I couldn't very well tell her I was making a grocery list while she was letting me in on everybody she loved.

> "And I love myself so much in the world. And I
> love the whole world. What else did you
> write down?"

Never mind. Later in the afternoon, Mom and Amy were talking about what to wear to Alex's birthday party –

> "Would you like to wear this dress tomorrow?"

> "No."

> "Oh Amy. Please, it's so pretty."

> "No."

> "Don't you like this dress? You are going to
> wear it to school, aren't you?"

> "Yes I like the dress, because I like you and I
> love you and I'm your best friend you."

When they start saying "love", the talking becomes a little soppy, doesn't it. What do you think of this –

> "Amy's gentle, kind, polite, thoughtful.
> Pleasant."

This is Amy's mom speaking, her exact words, all five of them. I wrote them down right away. A bit of soppiness from the little one and Mom melts.

My turn again. One evening at bedtime, I was more tired than Amy, and when I lay down with her she did most of the talking –

> "I love you. Do you know what? I love
> you."

Then she chuckled – chuckle, chuckle, chuckle – and went on –

"Do you know what? I said 'I love you, do you
know what, I love you'."

She chuckled some more, paused, and then concluded –

"Do you know what? I like your shirt."

So. This is a story about a brief time in the lives of an early four-year-old and a late two-year-old….about laughing and mush….about a very special love that begins abruptly, takes root, and grows warmly like the spring and summer seasons of our trip….and…. which of my shirts little Amy likes best. It's going to be exciting.

*   *   *   *   *

Does an almost-three-year-old have anything enlightening to say about "love"?

"Daddy. Do you want me to tell you this? I don't like you but I
love you."

Then he laughed and laughed. No, nothing enlightening. Not this one anyway. Alex's birthday parade is about to get underway, let's go watch.

Wednesday

These first few birthdays are so much fun and everyone wants to be part of them. The celebration becomes more of a process than an event. Amy's fourth was like that and here we go again. Alex will be three on Friday, today is Wednesday, and Grandma is having a family party tonight at her house. The kids can hardly wait, they're so excited.

Just a day or two ago, Jane mentioned to me that Alex is now at that age. At two, a toddler is too young to be concerned with birthday presents, but at three, the little one can't wait to get at them and rip them open in a big way. So we're all together at Grandma's and there are five gifts on the table. He knew they were for him, but he also knew we'd be telling him when he could open them. He was interested. With a little encouragement, he practiced counting with them. He seemed very much to be enjoying the fact that they were for him and that he was being centred out by it all. And he seemed patient.

Wait a minute – that's not Alex. What is he doing being patient at a time like this? What Jane said made sense, so why wasn't he after his presents? Why was he willing to have dinner first and birthday cake too? There must be a transition period when a child changes from unknowing indifference about gifts to uncaring wrapping-paper-destruction. It can't be more than a day or two. Maybe it happens on the third birthday itself. All of a sudden the little kid feels liberated and confident. We'll see what Alex does on Friday. I think the whole subject needs further investigation.

When we were home after the party, it was bedtime. Alex sure had a good time. He was very cute, it was fun being with him. I recalled talking to Amy about that at the cottage this summer. I lay down with her and asked her again why she thinks Alex is cute –

> "Only two reasons. He's funny and he talks funny. When he was counting his presents, he counted one-two on one present, two on one present, and then two on another, and three-four-five. He was funny counting his presents."

Actually, he was a real ham.

Thursday

Often these days Alex gets up just about the time I leave for work, and when he wakes he usually comes out of his bedroom right away. I love when I can tell him good morning with a hug and kiss. When he's up in time, he and Mom still go to the living room to "watch Daddy go out the window". Otherwise, I leave a little more quickly and almost always catch my bus.

Thursday morning, his birthday interest was more in line with what I'd expect, and very beautiful. I thought he was still asleep and was about to leave when Lynn asked if I wanted to see my birthday boy before going. I went back and peeked in. He wasn't sleeping at all; he was sitting on the floor with a couple of his gifts from the night before. He was so quiet and still a little slumberous, and I sat down beside him. I said –

"Do you like your presents?"

"Yes."

"Tomorrow is going to be your real birthday."

"Is it tomorrow yet?"

"No, it's today."

"Now it's today. But after today it's going to be tomorrow, and it's going to be my real birthday."

I thought about how he so often likes me to be the first to know about these matters that have just entered his mind. And I heard my bus drive off in the distance.

Alex's birthday parade paused Thursday evening. It will continue Friday at home, we've done our shopping and have some presents to give him on his real birthday. Then comes Saturday and we're going to the cottage – Kaitlyn and Lindsay, one more party. Madzy will be there too.

I thought I'd ask Alex to talk to me about his sister. Amy had just told me why she thinks Alex is cute, and that was very fun. Now it's Alex's turn, and when I had a chance, I asked him –

"Do you think Amy's cute?"

"Yes, the doll of Amy and my big sister Amy."

All right, I'd forgotten about Kristen's doll called "Amy". I'm pleased Alex thinks the doll is cute too, that's nice.

"So you think your big sister Amy is cute?"

"Yes."

"Why?"

"Because."

"Any other reasons?"

"Because. Because she loves me. SHE LOVES ME."

"Any other reasons?"

"No. Yes, Amy loves me. Let me tell you a secret."

He climbed all over my back and whispered in my ear –

"*Amy loves me.*"

"Any other reasons?"

"No. That's enough. I'm going to bed now, I'm not going to tell you
any more reasons."

That sure worked. All I had to do was ask him why Amy is cute and he was
as cute as can be. Off he went to bed.

Friday

"Guess what Daddy. I'm THREE!"

What a happy boy! I went to work with a smile on my face. Happy
Birthday boy!

It was difficult for him to wait through the day for my return. When
eventually I did arrive home, he asked me several times, "Where's my
presents?" Well, he'd had all day to think about that, and his memory from
Wednesday was still fresh. I evaded. Once, I said, "We're not going to
worry about your presents", and he replied, "Well where is them? You
could find them." Yes I could, and as soon as Lynn was home, I did.

He loves his yellow tiger. We'd bought him a big pillow, brown and shaped
like a dog. That one took more wrapping than all the others together. We
handed it to him. "This might be a big pillow" said Alex, and with some
help from Amy, tore open all that wrapping paper. One gift was a box of
clothes. He opened the box and I asked him –

"What do you think?"

"We should just close the box."

Which he did. Oh well. Such honesty – such sweet childishness.

What about the question from Grandma's party? How does a three-year-old
respond to being handed a carefully-wrapped gift? It seems that when there

are just Mom, Dad, and Amy around, he gets considerable help from his more experienced, wrapping-paper-destroying sister. Call it sibling interference, close the file, stamp it "Inconclusive", and – I don't care anyway. I'm going to the cottage.

*   *   *   *   *

Saturday and on

Off we went Saturday morning and it was a gorgeous drive. Summer is not quite finished yet. Neither is Alex's birthday – one party still to go and he's as excited as he was on Wednesday.

Soon after we arrived, I found him digging in a kitchen drawer –

"Look I found some tape!"

I suggested he just put it back because we didn't need to wrap presents today. He had something else in mind –

"No, when we have cake and ice cream, we can wrap it with this
and say 'Happy Birthday'."

Or maybe we could not wrap the cake and ice cream at all. Maybe we could just put some candles on it and leave it at that.

"It's okay for Amy to help blow out the candles because we're
both brothers and sisters."

The two of you blow them out? That ought to do it.

Madzy came, and just before lunch, Kaitlyn and Lindsay were at the door with Joy. More "Happy Birthday" wishes – indeed, that's the tradition – and we would have carried right on were it not for Kaitlyn. She had no birthday wish for Alex.

We didn't understand her hesitation and we all tried to coax a birthday greeting from her but with no success. It was time to call on the little man of the hour. He'd been an observer to this point but when we asked him to help, he said to Kaitlyn, "Say Happy Birthday" and right away Kaitlyn said, "Happy Birthday Alex." She just needed proper authorization. Now we could proceed with the party.

We gave Alex his presents and I read him the card that was with his gift from Madzy. Just as I finished, he looked her right in the eye and piped up –

"It's from you Madzy!"

He was right, it was from Madzy, and now she knew that too. He was right, he was happy, he was cute, fun, excited – he was three! He's half again as old as he had been a year earlier. He's aging quickly, isn't he. He's an old little boy.

Awhile later, Madzy had something for me too. It was a hug and a pat on the back and "Congratulations on your little boy." Yes, *my* little boy. I sensed a tear in my eye. I remembered that early April evening four-and-a-half years ago when it all began. There were many tears then. I recalled hearing "Congratulations" and wondering why, what had I done. But now, young Alex is three years away from his birth and I've done a lot. I'm still not sure I deserve it. I'm confused. When she said congratulations, it felt good. I'm proud of my little boy. Thanks Madzy.

Far away I hear the fading whistle of our train. It's gone now. Our summertime ride is over and the magic years are winding down. Don't you wish they'd go on? They can't of course. Growing is what's going on, and it's going on everywhere.

How much longer can I expect a little one to climb on my lap at the end of a pleasant restaurant dinner, not to help me with my dessert but to play with my glasses? Or maybe my nose? How much longer will we have two in the tub side-by-side on their tummies, sloshing from end to end and saying "Zzaa" in unison each time they change direction? We stopped playing the "Walk on Daddy's face" this summer. That had to happen but when it did, there was reluctance all around: it was so much fun once upon a time. Was this the defining moment when they ceased being little kids? No, there are many such moments as the magic slips away.

Recently, very politely, I asked Amy to stop growing. I even used words that I know she loves to use herself –

"Guess what Amy. Do you know what? I love you just the way
   you are. I don't want you to grow anymore. Just stay like
   you are. Okay?"

"Well I can't stop growing. I don't know how."

Oh no! She doesn't know how! What will we do? We'll teach her, we'll get
a tutor. We'll take her off food. Oh no! Please, Amy, please....

They grow, and their facial expressions begin to lose the spontaneity that
was so naturally theirs. The straight-line congruence between thought and
expression begins to bend. "No guile at all" doesn't always hold anymore.
They learn behaviour and it often comes out seeming other than natural.
They learn to fib a little, maybe a little white lie – maybe an enormously
blatant one if necessary. Sure they're still cute, they're still funny, still
warm, they're your children, they hardly ever lie, and they're beautiful!
But it's different. The magic isn't there anymore. The constancy is missing.

Have you noticed the cognitive growth of words and concepts? Amy is far
ahead of Alex here and almost ready to stop being a little kid altogether.
She's just learned too much to be able to hang in with him any longer.

Alex is so funny. And when Amy was his age, she was funny too. I
remember that well. At one time or another, I've been sure that each would
be a comedian one day. As they grow though, little ones come to know
much more about the meaning of words than they did when they first
started using them. As the gaps in their understanding close, usage
becomes adult, and the unexpected humour becomes conspicuous by its
absence.

It's the same with concepts. Alex will never mention the other moon at the
cottage again. We told him there's just the one. When we gave Amy a
globe and pointed out some cities and other places she knew, all Alex
wanted to know was its whereabouts. His only question, "Where's the
moon Daddy?" That was funny. So we told him about that too, and I don't
think he'll ever mention that again either. Day by day the magic wanes as
the knowledge pieces are put in place and the gaps fill up.

No, it's not likely that my son will be a comedian after all. Not when he
grows up anyway. The humour is a function of the process, and the process
is constrained by time. But he's full of it now and I sure do enjoy it – it's

magic, and it ain't over yet. Where is the little boy anyway? Excuse me while I go see what he's up to.

*   *   *   *   *

Two years now have gone by since we left Alex's long birthday party, two years since that Saturday morning at the cottage.

Three-year-old Alex was superb. Conversations with another four-year-old just carried right on. And still today, while he'll take his sword or a stack of books to bed with him, when I look in later on – likely as not it's good ol' Blacks Eyes who will be cuddled up next to him.

On the other hand, Amy is no longer a little kid. She stopped being cute one day when she was about five-and-a-half. You can call her beautiful – she'll smile. You can tell her she's such a sweet princess and she'll beam. You can tell her she's radiant and she'll smile radiantly even though she has no idea what radiant means. But, "You're cute Amy" prompts the following every time: "I am not cute!" She's too old for that I suppose.

A couple of evenings ago, I was sitting at the table with my pencil and some notes in front of me. I was thinking of the magic years. Amy was across the room and yes, she looked like a princess, though bigger than the one I was remembering. I asked her one more time to stop growing. "Daddy you're weird", she said. Oh. Another gap filled. It's time to stop being so, I suppose.

Then she came over and asked me, "Daddy, is that your book about how to be an adult when your children are five?" Yes, something like that. It's finished now. Thanks for coming along. The train ride was far more than exciting. If I could pick any part of my life to relive, this would be it, and I can't imagine that that will ever change. Have you been on other trips like this? Have you ever been on one where you were the mom or dad? Another train, another time, a different direction, but I'll bet it was every bit as "far more than exciting". Little kids sure are cute, aren't they. Goodbye.

EPILOGUE

"Guess what. I never change dreams, I just keep going on. Clown dreams and clown dreams and clown dreams and clown dreams and clown dreams and clown dreams and clown dreams and clown dreams...."

"....and clown dreams. I love clowns, they make me laugh so much. And guess what Amy. I love you too."

My how I love my little daughter.

*　　*　　*　　*　　*

Why are little kids cute? They really are you know – it's love. Yes, of course their faces are cute, pretty well all of them are. Together with other early-on attributes – the noises they make, their movement – you have an unarguable treatise for little-kid cuteness. And then there's the enormous amount of humour and warmth, emanating from the melding of bit-by-bit learning with a fresh, innocent, callow personality. This is unbelievably cute. But amidst all of this, a love is born. It grows quickly and closes your eyes as fairy dust turns it into magic.

Yes, it's love – one more fine reason why little kids are cute. But it's not a reason like the beautiful facial aesthetics, nor is it like the funny warm things they say and do. It's not what they present day in day out, but rather, it's a parent's response to their presentation. Excitement is heightened by love, and your little one just couldn't be any cuter.

In the beginning it's a crazy sort of love, but what could be expected of something that begins the way it does. And just when does a parent's love begin? Is it suddenly at birth in the middle of the night in a strange hospital? Or is it a few weeks later once you've come to know the new one? Maybe you've had a chance to check out the timbre of the wailing. Or, is it even some time before the child is born? Imagine that.

Anyway, you meet your kid and you're in love. It's a little work of art, isn't it – you created it and it's beautiful. Ask your mom and dad. Close friends come by and tell you it's beautiful too so it must be. Your love is digging in. Everyone who is important to you says congratulations and tells you your little one is fantastic. Of course you love it. It's terrifically cute and it doesn't matter what it looks like.

Then comes a phenomenon that has been passed down since the beginning. An otherwise healthy adult finds herself or himself saying things like "Kitchy-kitchy-coo" in public. Ever done it? It's an expression that one first hears as an infant, but likely never uses until now as a parent. Now you use it, aren't you glad you paid attention. Don't forget though, it's always delivered with accompanying facial contortions so be careful you don't get a cramp. It's intended to elicit a smile, a reaction of any sort from your little one. Your kid is in an uneducated, impulsive, totally non-self-conscious space, and as a parent you move right in. Your kid calls the shots. This isn't love – this is craziness. It's total infatuation and love can wait.

But it doesn't. Underneath, growing all the while, are the roots of your love for your child, firmly planted forever. It's a spring and summer growth and its blossoms indeed are the best. What love is stronger than that of a parent. And your little one's love for you, so manifest in its utter dependency, displayed daily with such grand enthusiasm, seems much the same. It's really very mutual.

Your child needs your love so much and it's so easy to give. "Congratulations" on your new baby girl, or on your three-year-old boy, simply are not deserved because of all the excitement you're having, all the fun, because of the incredible love that you feel. Little conversations like this can happen any time with any four-year-old. Amy said –

"You're the most wonderful mom in the whole world."

"Wow. How did I get to be such a good mommy?"

"Because we take care of each other every day."

Every single day.

It's a time in your life when you enjoy enormous emotional fulfillment, perhaps more than ever before or after. Clearly, undeniably, your life has real meaning. It's magnificent to watch and wonder as your children first learn to grasp their world. Because they are so unique, so funny, so very much yours in their early years, you feel a wonderful warmth. When you're not laughing at them, it melts you pure and simple and turns you into mush. It's magnificent to feel your love grow. A little crazy and giddy for now, your love reflects the crazy comments of your child, the fresh ones, the unexpected ones, the ones from imagination.

But the lustre of the magic will fade. Infatuation mellows – how could anything so wild continue – and newness yields to familiarity. It's expected. Wide-eyed innocent faces begin to show perspective and even maturity, if this can be said of ones as young as four or five. It's welcome. Their chosen words suggest this too, and it's not long before the essential learning is complete. Humour and warmth erupt much less frequently and it's sad. Far too soon the magic is gone and with reluctance and resignation one says goodbye, and your child? Yes – *your* child?

> "Say goodbye little one. It's time to go to school. It's time to learn to read and to write and that your friends are for everything and not just play. But they won't tell you how cute you were when you were two or three or four, nor how natural and absolutely beautiful was your response to your world. Your teachers won't tell you either, and you may never know. But you were and it was incredible, they were magic years and....you....were the magic. It's so true.

> "Learn this, and some far off day when you do, if you do, come back. When you were four, you were a wonderful little person and everybody thought so. Please come back. Do come back."

They have a physical presence with aesthetics and expressiveness found nowhere else. Their cognitive presentation, spontaneous and ever changing, is filled with humour and warmth. And, they inspire a love that becomes rock-solid and forever, but is somewhat crazy in the early going.

And that is when for a very small number of years, they are little kids. And that's why little kids are cute.

*　　*　　*　　*　　*

I think it began when he weighed about 23 pounds. He must be 30 pounds now but we're still doing it, and have done so maybe five or six times all told. In fact, we did it again just last night. It's a little routine that Alex and I have, and he's always the one to begin –

"When I get uppy, I be bigger than you."

Or is it: "….me be bigger than you", or maybe, "When me be uppy, me be bigger than you." My young son needs some schooling in his grammar. Anyway, I respond naturally enough –

"No you won't."

And we're underway. Our discussion proceeds –

"Yes, I will."

"No you won't."

"Yes."

"No."

"Want to see?"

"Okay."

And I reach under his arms and lift him up and hold him tightly against me with the top of his head two or three inches higher than the top of mine. Once settled and holding very still, we both take stock of the comparison, and he says –

"See?!!!"

And I say –

"Oh no, you ARE bigger than me."

He laughs. His nose is so small and cute. And his beautiful eyes sparkle as he laughs and laughs and laughs. And his ever-so-fine hair feels so soft on my face as down he comes. Still he laughs. And it's so infectious, how can I not laugh too. We both laugh and I feel so warm inside. I love you so much Alex. I love you and I love you and I love you and I love you and I love you and I love you....

Tony has been a writer all his life, although his chosen profession lies elsewhere. He taught accounting at the University of the West Indies in Jamaica and also at Carleton University in Ottawa. He wrote a text for his first-year students that was well received – an "explanatory" approach to introductory accounting. He was the Project Finance Officer with CUSO, a Canadian NGO, where descriptive procedure manuals were required. He wrote these, and they too were very welcome and used effectively.

Scott and Danny have passed on. Another golden, Corey Renoir, is his canine companion nowadays. A long walk on a country road is a favourite pastime for both. Tony still likes to stop at Silver Lake for a break from the traffic or an along-the-way snack. Or – just to relax and remember that summer trip years ago with two little ones. He enjoys darts in a league at the Black Sheep Inn in Wakefield, Québec, and that's him in the picture trying on his new darts hoody, what do you think?

Tony lives with his family by a small lake in the Gatineau Hills, an hour north of Ottawa.

Email address - anthony@byebyeandrocketcandies.com
Website - www.byebyeandrocketcandies.com

Photograph by - Stuart David

.

.

Made in the USA
Charleston, SC
05 December 2013